T0402381

THE FIELD GUIDE TO EMBROIDERY

52 NORTH AMERICAN ANIMAL & PLANT DESIGNS FOR NATURE LOVERS

JESSICA KEMPER

SCHIFFER
CRAFT
4880 Lower Valley Road • Atglen, PA 19310

Other Schiffer Craft Books on Related Subjects:

PixlPeople: Cross-Stitch Your Favorite People, John-Michael Stoof, ISBN 978-0-7643-6191-3

Juno's Nature Embroidery Notebook: Stitching Plants, Animals, and Stories, Juno, ISBN 978-0-7643-6422-8

Embroidery Garden: Artful Designs Inspired by Nature, Yanase Rei, ISBN 978-0-7643-6424-2

Library of Congress Control Number: 2024941457

Designed by Llara Pazdan
Typeset by Lori Malkin Ehrlich
Cover design by Llara Pazdan
Diagrams on page 22 by Mollie Johanson
Type set in Journal OT / Museo Sans

ISBN: 978-0-7643-6916-2
ePub: 978-1-5073-0562-1
Printed in India

MIX
Paper | Supporting responsible forestry
FSC
www.fsc.org
FSC™ C016779

Published by Schiffer Craft
An imprint of Schiffer Publishing, Ltd.
4880 Lower Valley Road
Atglen, PA 19310
Phone: (610) 593-1777; Fax: (610) 593-2002
Email: Info@schifferbooks.com
Web: www.schifferbooks.com

To our beloved North American wildlife.
From insects to mammals, birds, and reptiles,
you inspire my curiosity in nature
and creativity on a daily basis.

Acknowledgments

Thanks to my partner, Kyle, who reviewed in detail every pattern in this book. I'd also like to thank our two rescue dogs, Pickle June and Phoebe, for always being around to remind me to take breaks and go outside to play.

And thank you to those of you who are putting in the work to ensure there is a future for the wildlife we all love so dearly. Whether you're working in conservation, rehabilitation, city planning, volunteer efforts, or in so many other ways, including those of you making wildlife art, this book is for all of you.

Contents

Preface 12
Introduction 15
How to Use This Guide 24
Ecosystems Key 25

Section 1: Desert 26

28 **Gila Monster**
Heloderma suspectum

30 **Turkey Vulture**
Cathartes aura

32 **Desert Plant Trio**
(saguaro cactus, Mojave prickly pear cactus, Mojave yucca)
Carnegiea gigantea, Opuntia erinacea, Yucca schidigera

34 **Black-Tailed Jackrabbit**
Lepus californicus

36 **Arizona Bark Scorpion**
Centruroides sculpturatus

38 **Desert Tortoise**
Gopherus agassizii

40 **Ringtail**
Bassariscus astutus

42 **Greater Roadrunner**
Geococcyx californianus

Section 2: Mountain 44

46 **Boreal Toad**
Anaxyrus boreas boreas

48 **Mountain Goat**
Oreamnos americanus

50 **American Pika**
Ochotona princeps

52 **Mountain Lion**
Puma concolor

54 **Elk**
Cervus canadensis

56 **Mountain Wildflower Mix**
(western coneflower, common yarrow, paintbrush, silvery lupine, showy fleabane)
Rudbeckia occidentalis, Achillea millefolium, Castilleja coccinea, Lupinus argenteus, Erigeron speciosus

58 **Bighorn Sheep**
Ovis canadensis

60 **Grizzly Bear**
Ursus arctos horribilis

Section 3: Waterways 62

64 **Eastern Newt**
Notophthalmus viridescens

66 **Osprey**
Pandion haliaetus

68 **Common Loon**
Gavia immer

70 **American Beaver**
Castor canadensis

72 **North American River Otter**
Lontra canadensis

74 **Sockeye Salmon**
Oncorhynchus nerka

76 **American Alligator**
Alligator mississippiensis

Section 4: Forest 78

80 **Moose**
Alces alces

82 **Black Bear**
Ursus americanus

84 **Gray Wolf**
Canis lupus

86 **Barred Owl**
Strix varia

88 **Little Brown Bat**
Myotis lucifugus

90 **Downy Woodpecker**
Picoides pubescens

92 **Spruce Twigs**
Picea glauca

Section 5: Ocean 94

96 **Orca**
Orcinus orca

98 **Ochre Sea Star**
Pisaster ochraceus

100 **Florida Manatee**
Trichechus manatus latirostris

102 **Gray Whale**
Eschrichtius robustus

104 **Green Sea Turtle**
Chelonia mydas

106 **Great White Shark**
Carcharodon carcharias

108 **Tufted Puffin**
Fratercula cirrhata

Section 6: Prairie

Section 6: Prairie 110

112 **American Bison**
Bison bison

114 **Utah Prairie Dog**
Cynomys parvidens

116 **Black-Footed Ferret**
Mustela nigripes

118 **Pronghorn**
Antilocapra americana

120 **Red-Winged Blackbird**
Agelaius phoeniceus

122 **American Badger**
Taxidea taxus

124 **Greater Sage Grouse**
Centrocercus urophasianus

126 **Prairie Wildflower Mix**
(swamp milkweed, prairie goldenrod)
with monarch butterfly
Asclepias incarnata, Solidago nemoralis,
Danaus plexippus

Section 7: Urban 128

130 Coyote
Canis latrans

132 Common Raccoon
Procyon lotor

134 Common Garter Snake
Thamnophis sirtalis

136 Red Fox
Vulpes vulpes

138 American Herring Gull
Larus smithsonianus

140 Striped Skunk
Mephitis mephitis

142 Red-Tailed Hawk
Buteo jamaicensis

Preface

The environment and art have been intertwined since the beginning of time. Both offer inspiration, creativity, and relaxation. In this book I intend to "stitch" together ecosystem intricacies through hand-stitched embroidery, emphasizing flora, fauna, and landscapes native to North America.

Nature is a place where you can find solitude, connection, and wonder. As ever increasing numbers of people flock to national and city parks in search of refuge, this book offers a way to pay homage to the spaces that have become so beloved. In these places we face ourselves and our thoughts, emotions, and challenges. Among us we find wildlife and plant species who are facing their own challenges of population decline by way of invasive species, climate change, habitat fragmentation, pollution, and so on. I find it incredibly therapeutic to create art on these topics when I'm plagued by the question "Well, what can I do to help?"

My partner and I found ourselves enamored of the natural landscape and inhabitants upon moving to the West. We spent weekends waking up before the sunrise to visit bird refuges, or driving up our cities' mountain canyons to catch a glimpse of a moose. We'd hike miles to see a mountain goat. We stopped and enjoyed every creature from grizzlies to wolves to chipmunks and robins.

Some of the best memories of my life are tied to encounters with wildlife. I have been deeply moved by many birds, whales, and beetles; some have been highlighted in this book. What an absolute treat it is to be able to respectfully share space with these resilient creatures. Embroidery has inspired me to relive many of these memories, by stitching the scene and trying to capture the emotion I felt at that moment in time.

While grand outdoor adventures can allow you to spot unique wildlife, I want to be clear that you don't have to live somewhere "special" to enjoy nature. Nature is all around us, no matter how altered the environment is to suit human needs. Even now, living in Atlanta, we still find ourselves going for evening birding walks with our dogs. No matter where you live, there is wildlife all around you.

Throughout college and while working for years as a sustainability professional, I found myself experiencing what is known as ecological grief. This form of grief and anxiety is triggered by climate-change-related loss and can cause long-term feelings of despair. Unnaturally hot wildfires, pollution, habitat fragmentation, invasive species, and more contribute to population and resiliency decline of wildlife populations. If you are here because you appreciate wildlife, or you work in wildlife ecology and research, or you are just becoming interested, I'd like to thank you. Working toward large conservation goals isn't always straightforward, but with folks like you caring, there is a better chance for a positive outcome.

My embroidery business, Field Guide Embroidery, came about because I needed a way to express my eco-grief. I started by stitching thrifted flannel shirts in my free time, then I started attending markets, being accepted to art shows, and building a beautiful community of nature lovers. Field Guide Embroidery continued to grow as I worked to bring attention to animals that were in decline, and to raise funds for environmental and wildlife nonprofits doing incredible work and research. Connecting with many people over their love of a species I've stitched over the years has brought me so much joy. I have loved and cherished every story shared with me about a memory of seeing an animal in the wild.

This beautiful community of people also sparked the idea to write this book. My goal is to empower you to express your eco-grief through art. Stitch your favorite animal on a hat and wear it with pride. Feel excited when someone asks you what kind of salamander that is on your sweatshirt. We are in this together!

If you haven't already, I encourage you to do a quick search of what organizations in your area are doing work for our natural world. It is hard work, and they often need all the help they can get. This can be by way of donation, sharing a post on social media, or volunteering. Not only will you have a one-of-a-kind experience, but I promise you will meet some of the kindest, most genuine people.

Introduction

How to Use This Book

The seven chapters of this book are sorted into Desert, Mountain, Waterways (rivers and lakes), Forest, Ocean, Prairie, and Urban. The chapters contain several animal and plant projects that are found in that ecosystem. The animals listed within each ecosystem may live in a variety of ecosystems, but they've been categorized this way on the basis of my own experiences of viewing or learning about them. Each project shows a photo of the finished product, a traceable pattern, and a stitching guide with the stitches and corresponding colors of embroidery thread to use.

Some of the animals featured in this book are considered threatened to critically endangered, such as the black-footed ferret, boreal toad, and desert tortoise. I have always been very drawn to these species facing decline and unaware that so many of us are rooting for them. Other animals featured in this book are not declining to the same degree but were chosen because they are simply iconic (such as the red fox, black bear, and downy woodpecker). No matter their classification, all of these wild creatures are magical. It's time to dive in to the projects!

Preparing to Embroider

Getting Started

Embroidery can seem daunting, but I promise that while it's time consuming, it is rewarding. Throughout this book you'll find patterns that range from easy to challenging. Jump in wherever you feel most comfortable, based on the number of stitch types used or the complexity of the pattern. In this introduction, we'll go over all of my tips and tricks to getting started, supplies needed, and methods for stitching.

How to Choose an Item to Embroider

I most commonly stitch on functional items, like clothes, hats, and shoes. I find that not only is it a cost-effective way to refresh my wardrobe, but fashion can be a wasteful industry, so I like to use items that would otherwise be discarded. You can find a great pair of shoes or an old hat at a thrift store, clothing swap, or maybe even in your closet. If stitching on clothes isn't something you are interested in, no problem! I have also stitched fabric that later turned into wall art. There are endless possibilities for projects, as long as you consider a few things.

While choosing what you'd like to embroider, the most important part is to consider the integrity of the material you will be adorning. For example, waterproof materials are not the best choice, because by piercing the material with a needle you will no longer have an item that is waterproof. You'll also want to consider the pliability of the material. If you choose a very thick material, such as leather, you will find yourself moving a lot slower than anticipated because it's hard to push a needle through something that thick! Jean jackets, felt hats, flannel shirts, cotton in general, and boots with elastic panels all are excellent mediums to start with. When considering if you should embroider something, remind yourself that you'll be piercing it with a needle over a hundred times; can the material withstand that and will you be able to complete the entire project while having fun?

Materials

While there are many methods to embroidery, here is the method that works best for me.

ITEMS YOU WILL NEED TO START EMBROIDERING:

- An item to embroider
- Embroidery floss
- A needle
- Scissors
- Stabilizer
- Writing utensil that washes out (a pencil, colored pencil, etc.; avoid permanent markers)

ITEMS THAT CAN BE NICE TO HAVE:

- A magnetic needle minder
- Iron-on protective backing
- Embroidery hoop
- Thimble

EMBROIDERY FLOSS

There are several brands of embroidery floss. My favorite, and likely the most accessible, is a brand called DMC, found at most craft stores. Each color of thread is given a unique number, and you will see it on the label of the skein. Those numbers are listed on each pattern in the book, so you know which colors to purchase.

NEEDLE

Again, I recommend the brand DMC, and I use a needle specific for embroidery (#5). Whatever needle you use, it needs to have an eye that is large enough to string your embroidery threads. General sewing needles can be very challenging to thread because the eyes can be small.

STABILIZER

I stitch exclusively using a stabilizer. The purpose of a stabilizer is to hold your material in a constant state, so that it does not

stretch or pull in a way that would warp your fabric upon completion. For example, it's extremely useful if you want to embroider a soft cotton shirt where you could accidentally pull stitches too tight without knowing it, thus ruining your T-shirt by causing unfortunate puckering. The brands Sulky and Pellon are two great options that come in a large roll or individual sheets. An added bonus is that stabilizer makes pattern transfer a breeze (see below).

IRON-ON PROTECTIVE BACKING

You can purchase a material that can be ironed onto the back of your creation to protect your skin from the rough stitching on the back. This is also often called stabilizer. While not necessary, it's useful if you are stitching children's clothes, or clothes that will have direct skin contact.

EMBROIDERY HOOP

I use a hoop for some projects, but not others. Use of stabilizer makes using a hoop unnecessary in most cases. If I am stitching a project that has a really soft drape to it, such as a flannel shirt, I will use a hoop to keep the fabric taut. If I am embroidering a hat, I will just use the stabilizer. See what works best for you!

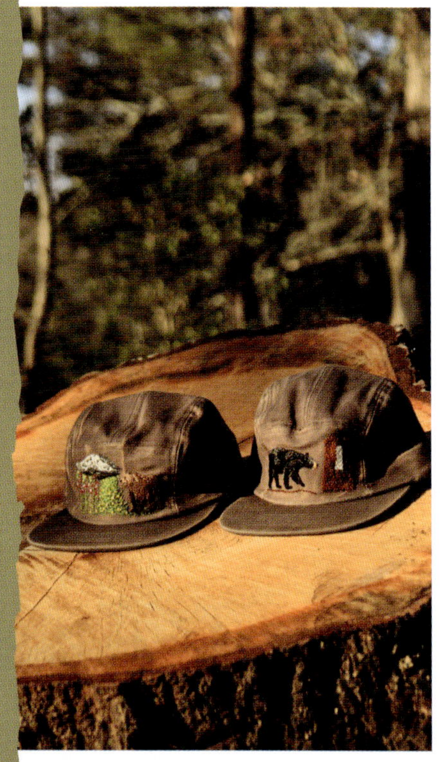

Stitch Methods: Tips for Stitching Animals, Fur, Feathers, Etc.

METHODS FOR TRANSFERRING YOUR PATTERN

Stabilizer is useful because you can trace your pattern directly onto the stabilizer, place it on your item of choice, and stitch from there. There are several kinds of stabilizer, and most have an adhesive to stick them onto your project. For stabilizers that are not adhesive, you'll need pins or tape.

Tearaway stabilizer and wash-away stabilizer each has its own place. For example, if you're stitching a felt hat that you don't want to get wet, use the tearaway stabilizer. For shirts, flannels, and cotton hats, the wash-away works well. I use an adhesive wash-away stabilizer for 90% of the projects I make.

To transfer your pattern, simply cut out a piece of stabilizer to size, place it over the pattern you'd like to use, and trace the lines with a washable writing utensil such as a ballpoint pen or pencil. Sometimes it can help to hold the page and stabilizer up to a bright window, or to put your phone flashlight under the book page to ensure you can see all the lines.

PREPARING EMBROIDERY FLOSS

The DMC floss used in this book comes in skeins of six twisted strands of embroidery thread. When you have gathered the thread colors you need (noted by number), you'll also see on each pattern that it states how many strands of thread you need. For example, many of the faces that require more detail use two strands of embroidery thread, while the body often uses three. At times it might be one of a certain color, mixed with two of another color. This is common since our wildlife species often have mottled fur or skin.

Start by pulling the loose thread on the end of the skein that has the larger label including the color number. That will minimize knotting. Pull a length of thread you feel comfortable working with. If you make it too long, you risk creating knots while stitching and your arm will fatigue; if too short, you'll be rethreading your needle constantly. I work in lengths of 10 to 12 inches on average.

Next, separate the six strands of thread. Even if you are preparing three strands of the same color, this is an important step because it will allow the threads to lie nice and flat within your project.

The first stitches, placed throughout the large area, guide its overall direction.

STITCHING

Some tips for your first few stitches on a project:

- Whenever I start stitching with a new thread, I refrain from knotting it to keep it in place on the back. Rather, I weave it into the backs of other stitches, or will hold the tail down with subsequent stitches. Because we are introducing so many sections of thread, knots can become troublesome and will keep your project from lying flat upon completion.
- It can be helpful to pick just one color to start with and stitch all of that at once. You can pull out plenty of thread, separate it, and repiece to the desired number of strands, and you'll then have them prepared for stitching. Having these threads prepared can help keep momentum moving on your project.
- When you finish your thread length, simply weave your needle through the backs of your stitches to hold it in place.

While you are working on your project:

- It can be helpful when starting a large section to use the first threads to outline the direction the stitches are going to be moving. I do this by placing stitches spaced out throughout the section in the intended direction, rather than stitching one solid block starting in a corner.
- After you lay down those general direction stitches, it's best to work in small sections, laying stitches close together to make the most of the length of your thread.
- While stitching, consider the animal you are working on. If it's a furry mammal, consider that fur is not always perfectly in line and straight. The stitch that I use for fur is a cross between straight and seed stitch. I like to place some stitches that are facing in opposing or random directions to imitate what fur would look like on a wild animal.

STITCH TYPES USED IN THIS BOOK

BACKSTITCH This stitch is often used to add a border to a section of stitching, or for flower stems. Backstitch creates a consistent straight line by lining single stitches up end to end.

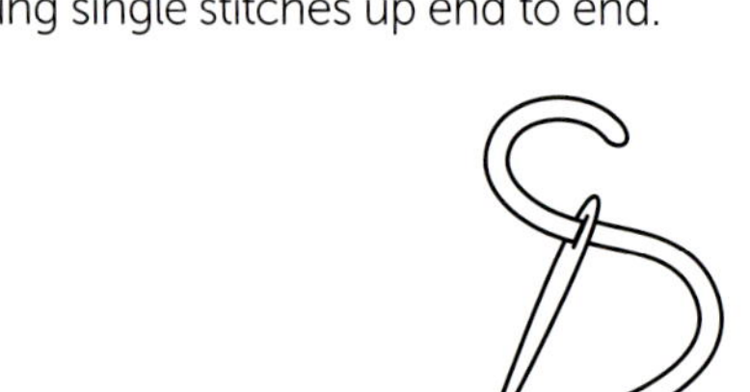
2
1
4
3

LAZY DAISY: This stitch is useful for small loops you are planning to make, like those on the lupine flowers included in the mountain wildflower mix pattern. You may also place three straight stitches alongside each other to create a similar effect.

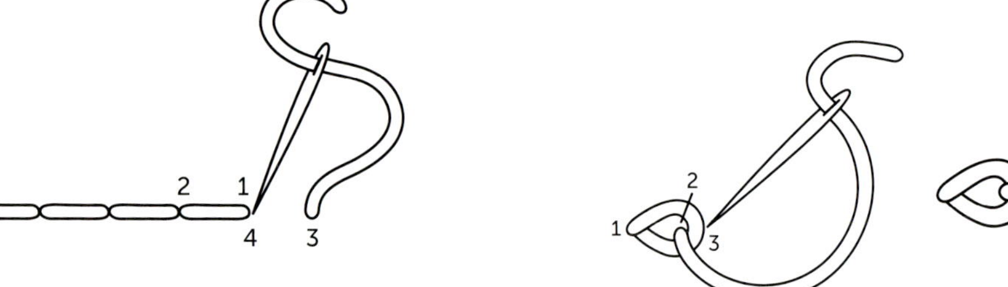
2
1
3

STRAIGHT STITCH: I use the straight stitch most commonly on projects needing stitches that all are moving in the same direction but are not randomized like fur stitch. Straight stitch is often used for animals that do not have fur, such as birds or fish.

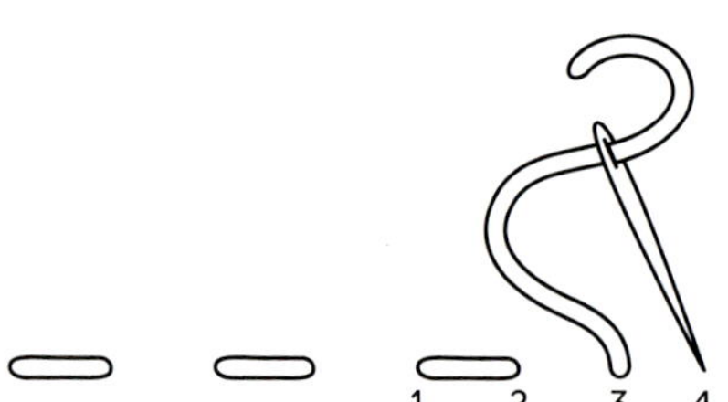
1
2
3
4

FRENCH KNOT: French knots are useful for little spots on animals or pupils of the eyes. You may find them useful on patterns such as the manatee or eastern newt, but they are optional since you can also just stitch a very small stitch to serve the same purpose.

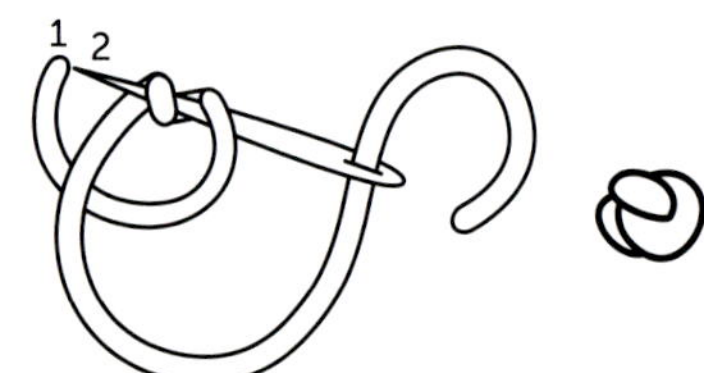
1
2

FUR STITCH: This stitch, a cross between straight and seed stitch, is what I devised to best convey the essence of animal fur. It can also be useful for feathers or other creature surface textures.

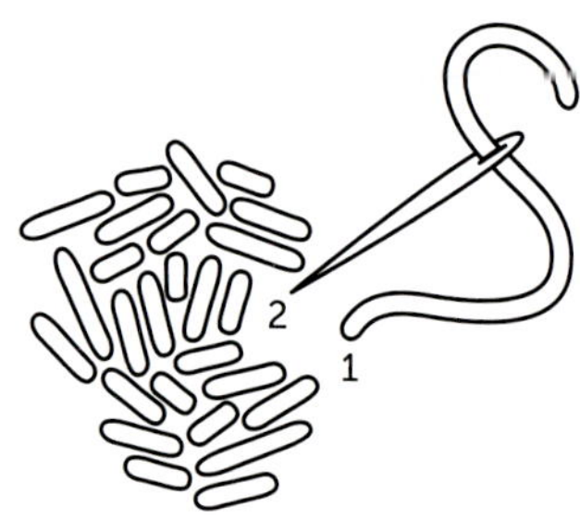
2
1

Finishing Your Project

Once you've completed the stitching portion of your project, it's time to remove the stabilizer so your item can be worn. Follow the directions for the type of stabilizer you have chosen and let it dry flat if you are rinsing with water. Once it's dry, ensure you are happy with your stitchwork and add any last details if they were accidentally missed.

If you wish to use an iron-on protective backing (see above), now is the time to apply it.

Caring for Your Embroidered Project

When I sell a piece of embroidery, I share with wearers that this type of embroidery is very hardy. I have projects that have gone through the washing machine and dryer dozens of times and still look great. Some of this will depend on the item you've chosen to embroider. Please follow the washing instructions for your chosen garment. If you really want to ensure preservation of your stitched work, wash your item on the delicate washing cycle and lay it flat to dry.

How to Use This Guide

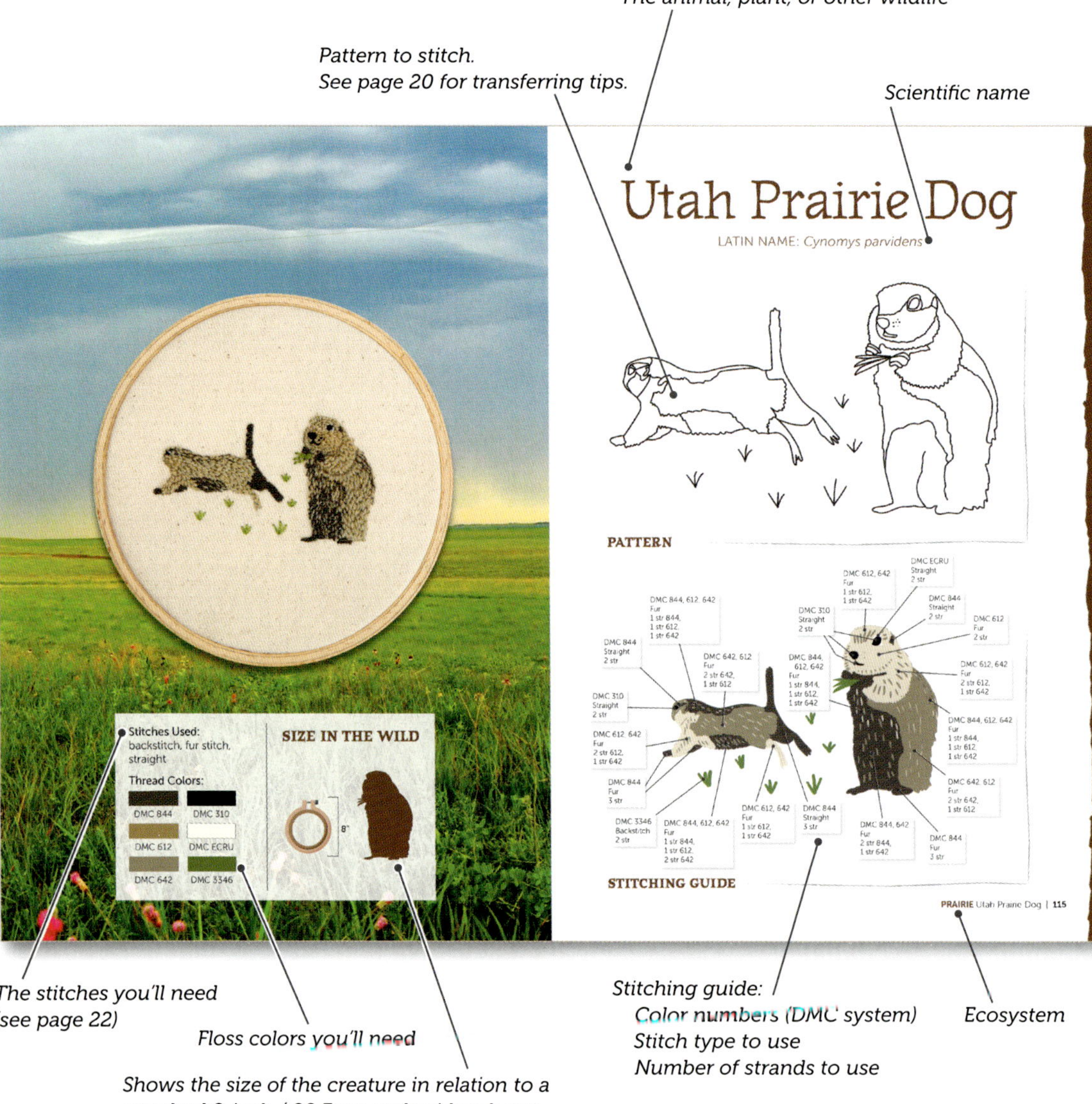
The animal, plant, or other wildlife
Pattern to stitch.
See page 20 for transferring tips.
Scientific name
Utah Prairie Dog
LATIN NAME: Cynomys parvidens
PATTERN
STITCHING GUIDE
Stitches Used:
backstitch, fur stitch, straight
Thread Colors:
DMC 844
DMC 310
DMC 612
DMC ECRU
DMC 642
DMC 3346
SIZE IN THE WILD
8"
PRAIRIE Utah Prairie Dog | 115
The stitches you'll need
(see page 22)
Floss colors you'll need
Shows the size of the creature in relation to a
standard 8-inch / 20.3 cm embroidery hoop
Stitching guide:
Color numbers (DMC system)
Stitch type to use
Number of strands to use
Ecosystem

Ecosystems Key

The wildlife in this book may live widely dispersed from their "typical" ecosystems. This key serves as a very general guide to help us better appreciate our ecosystems. The areas shown are representative of the six ecosystems listed.

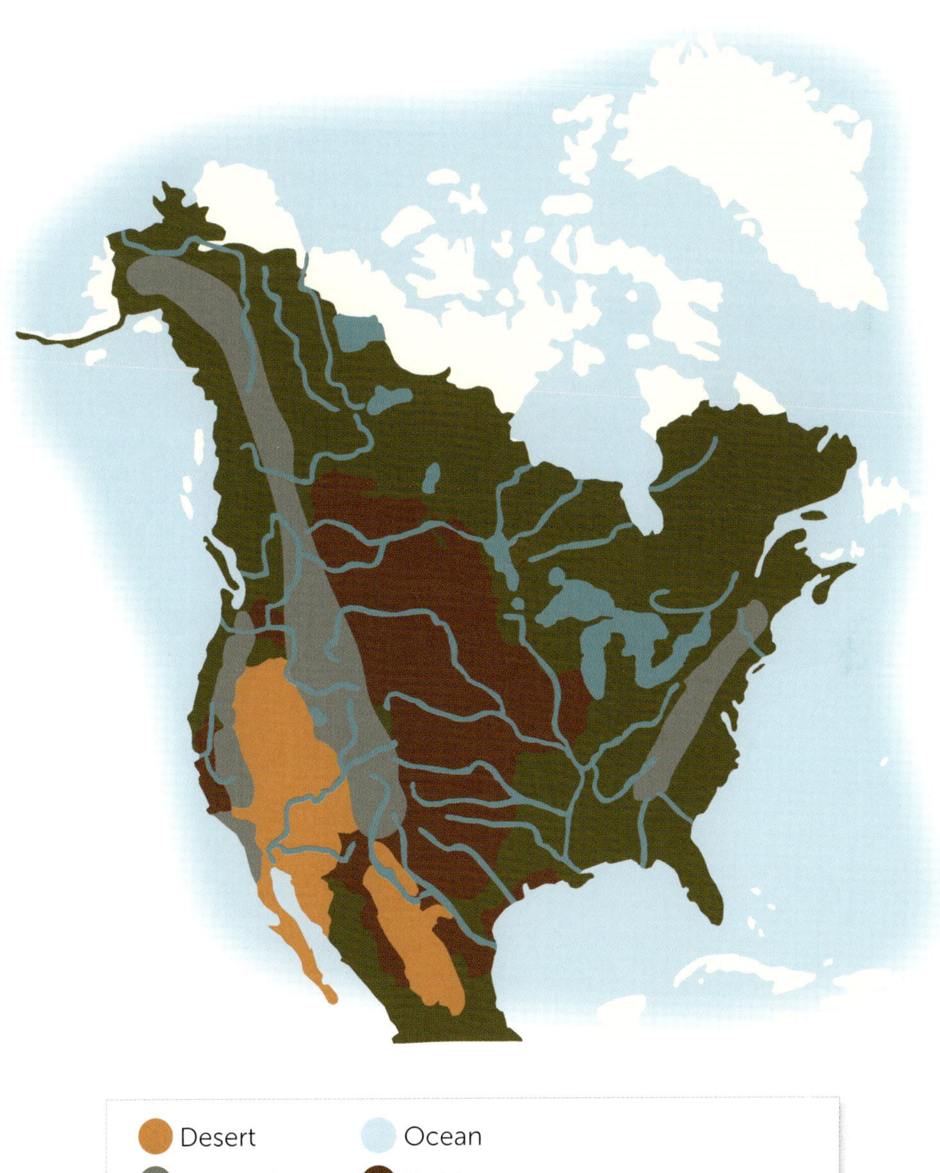

Desert
Mountain
Waterways
Forest
Ocean
Prairie
Urban: widely scattered throughout

Section I

DESERT

The North American desert ecosystem is home to a fascinating range of species that have evolved strategies to live in harsh conditions such as extreme temperatures, varied altitudes, and limited water availability. Often relying on nocturnal or fossorial (that is, underground) activity, desert wildlife species such as scorpions, Gila monsters, and desert tortoises can seem especially mysterious to us.

The three major desert areas of North America—the Sonoran, Mojave, and Chihuahuan—are in northern Mexico and the American Southwest.

Stitches Used:
backstitch, straight
Thread Colors:
DMC 310
DMC 722
DMC 3799
SIZE IN THE WILD
8"

Gila Monster

LATIN NAME: *Heloderma suspectum*

PATTERN

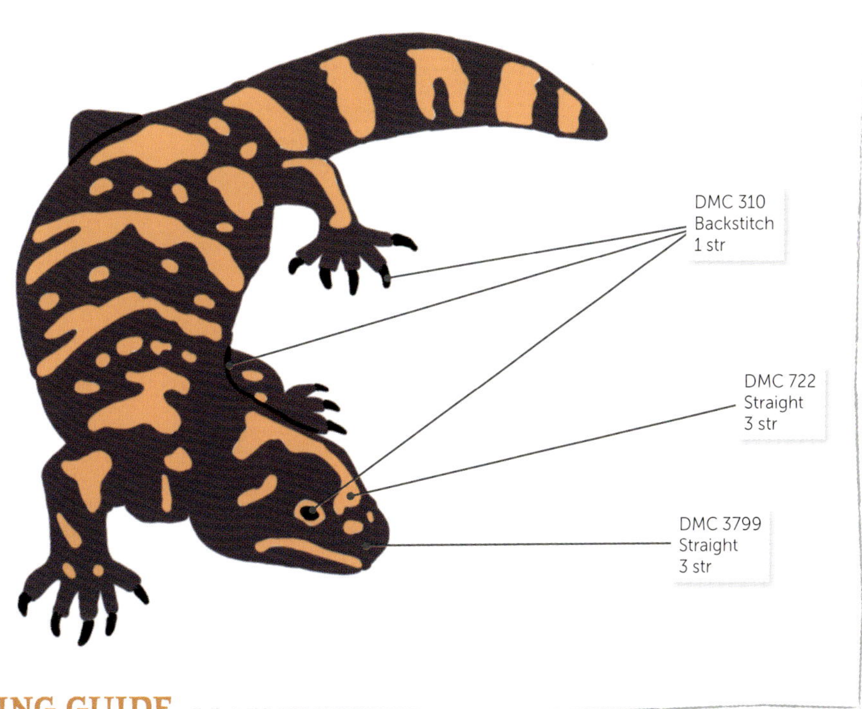
DMC 310
Backstitch
1 str
DMC 722
Straight
3 str
DMC 3799
Straight
3 str

STITCHING GUIDE

Stitches Used:
fur stitch, straight
Thread colors:
DMC 3782
DMC 938
DMC 356
DMC 535
DMC 310
DMC 3865
DMC 22
SIZE IN THE WILD
8"

Turkey Vulture

LATIN NAME: *Cathartes aura*

PATTERN

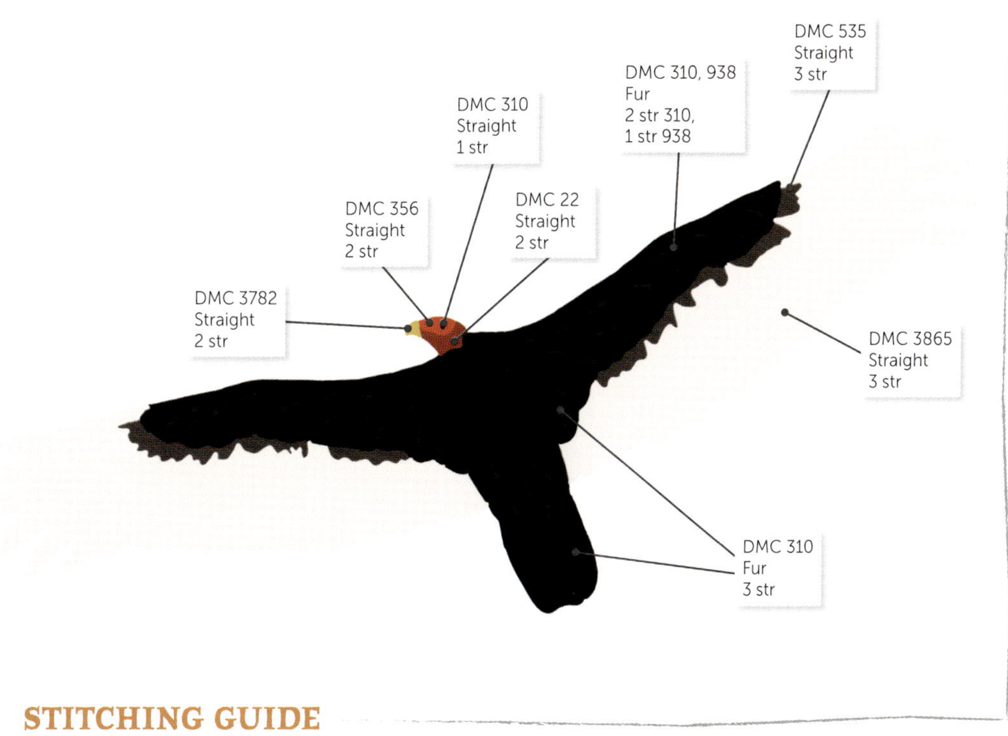
DMC 535
Straight
3 str
DMC 310, 938
Fur
2 str 310,
1 str 938
DMC 310
Straight
1 str
DMC 356
Straight
2 str
DMC 22
Straight
2 str
DMC 3782
Straight
2 str
DMC 3865
Straight
3 str
DMC 310
Fur
3 str

STITCHING GUIDE

Stitches Used:
backstitch, French knot, straight
Thread Colors:
DMC 936
DMC 937
DMC 726
DMC 3052
DMC 535
DMC 904
DMC 3866
SIZE IN THE WILD
8"

Desert Plant Trio

(saguaro cactus, Mojave prickly pear cactus, Mojave yucca)

LATIN NAMES: *Carnegiea gigantea, Opuntia erinacea, Yucca schidigera*

PATTERN

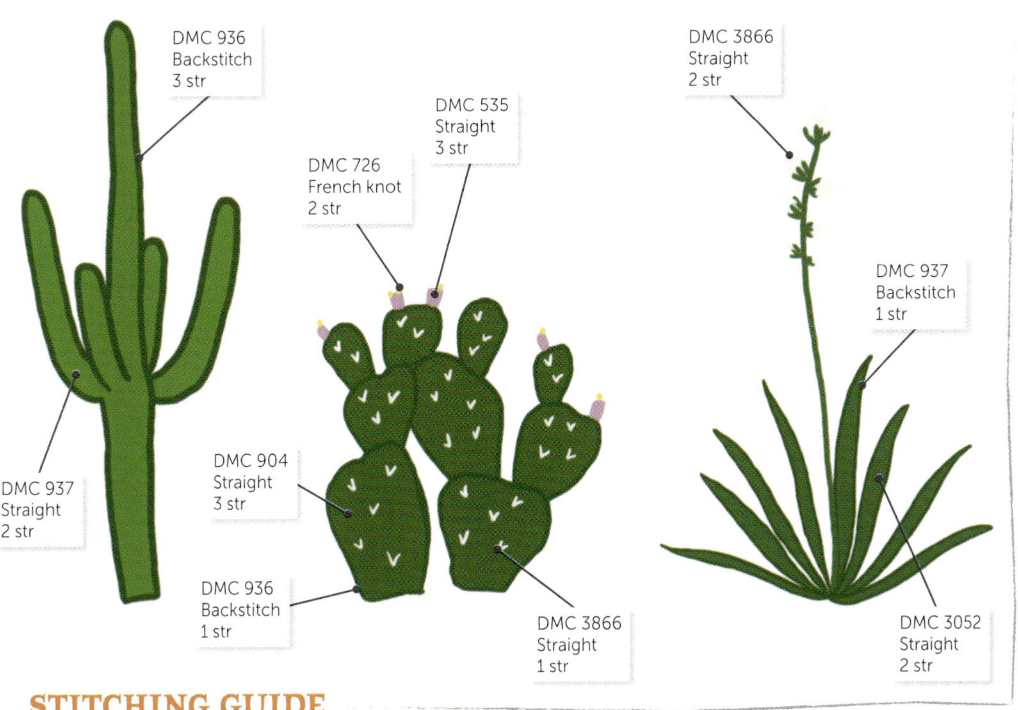

DMC 936
Backstitch
3 str
DMC 937
Straight
2 str
DMC 535
Straight
3 str
DMC 726
French knot
2 str
DMC 904
Straight
3 str
DMC 936
Backstitch
1 str
DMC 3866
Straight
1 str
DMC 3866
Straight
2 str
DMC 937
Backstitch
1 str
DMC 3052
Straight
2 str

STITCHING GUIDE

Stitches Used:
backstitch, fur stitch, straight
Thread Colors:
DMC 3799
DMC 729
DMC 3865
DMC 869
DMC 169
DMC 310
DMC 317
DMC 3778
SIZE IN THE WILD
8"

Black-Tailed Jackrabbit

LATIN NAME: *Lepus californicus*

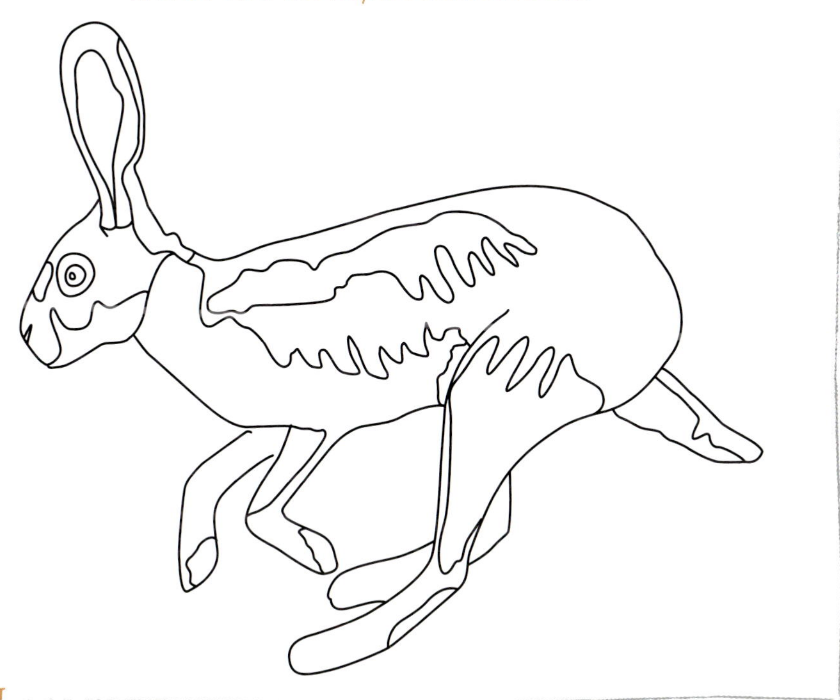

PATTERN

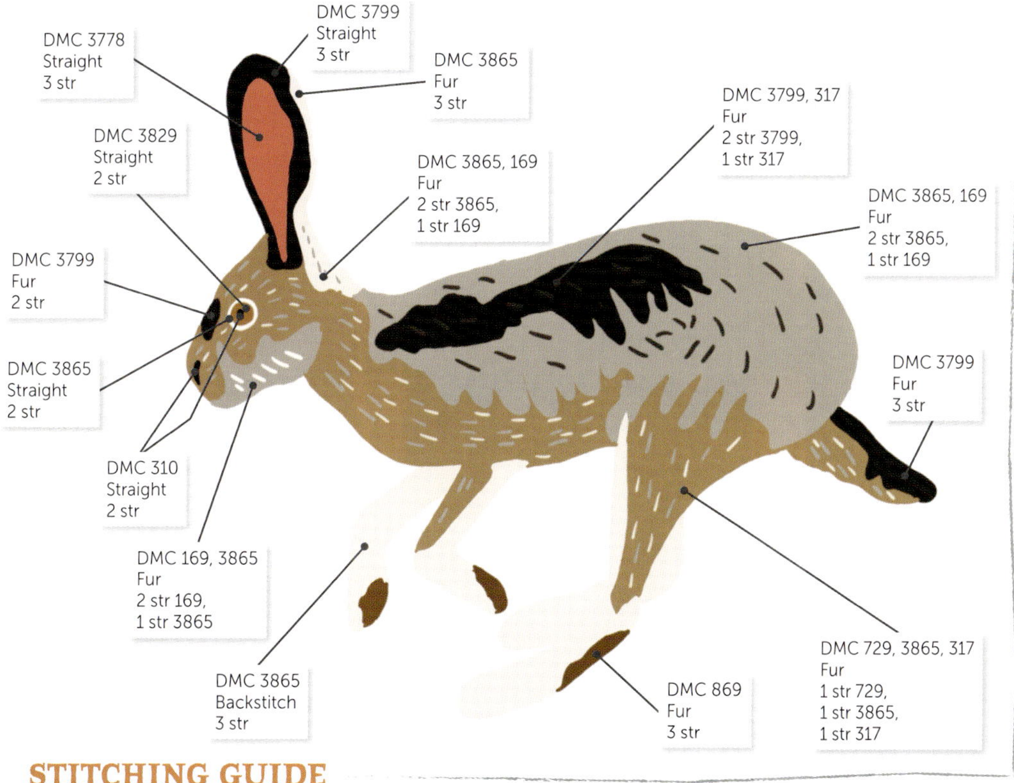
DMC 3778
Straight
3 str
DMC 3799
Straight
3 str
DMC 3865
Fur
3 str
DMC 3829
Straight
2 str
DMC 3865, 169
Fur
2 str 3865,
1 str 169
DMC 3799, 317
Fur
2 str 3799,
1 str 317
DMC 3865, 169
Fur
2 str 3865,
1 str 169
DMC 3799
Fur
2 str
DMC 3865
Straight
2 str
DMC 3799
Fur
3 str
DMC 310
Straight
2 str
DMC 169, 3865
Fur
2 str 169,
1 str 3865
DMC 3865
Backstitch
3 str
DMC 869
Fur
3 str
DMC 729, 3865, 317
Fur
1 str 729,
1 str 3865,
1 str 317

STITCHING GUIDE

Stitches Used:
backstitch, straight
Thread Colors:
DMC 646
DMC 729
DMC 3829
SIZE IN THE WILD
8"

Arizona Bark Scorpion

LATIN NAME: *Centruroides sculpturatus*

PATTERN

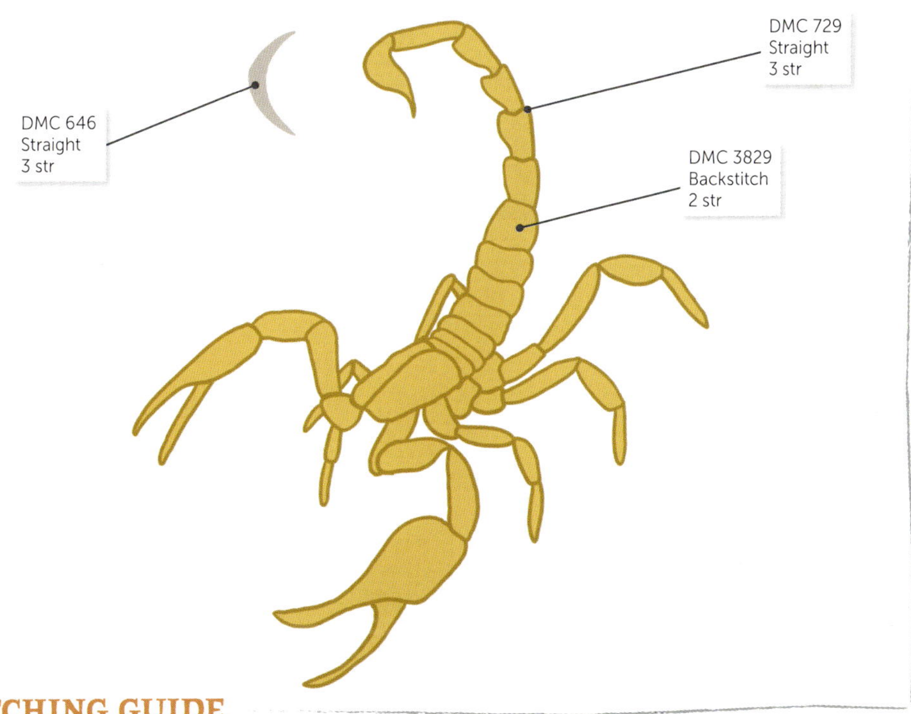
DMC 729
Straight
3 str
DMC 646
Straight
3 str
DMC 3829
Backstitch
2 str

STITCHING GUIDE

Stitches Used:
backstitch, straight
Thread Colors:
DMC 732
DMC 829
DMC 310
DMC 3781
DMC 3012
DMC 433
SIZE IN THE WILD
8"

Desert Tortoise

LATIN NAME: *Gopherus agassizii*

PATTERN

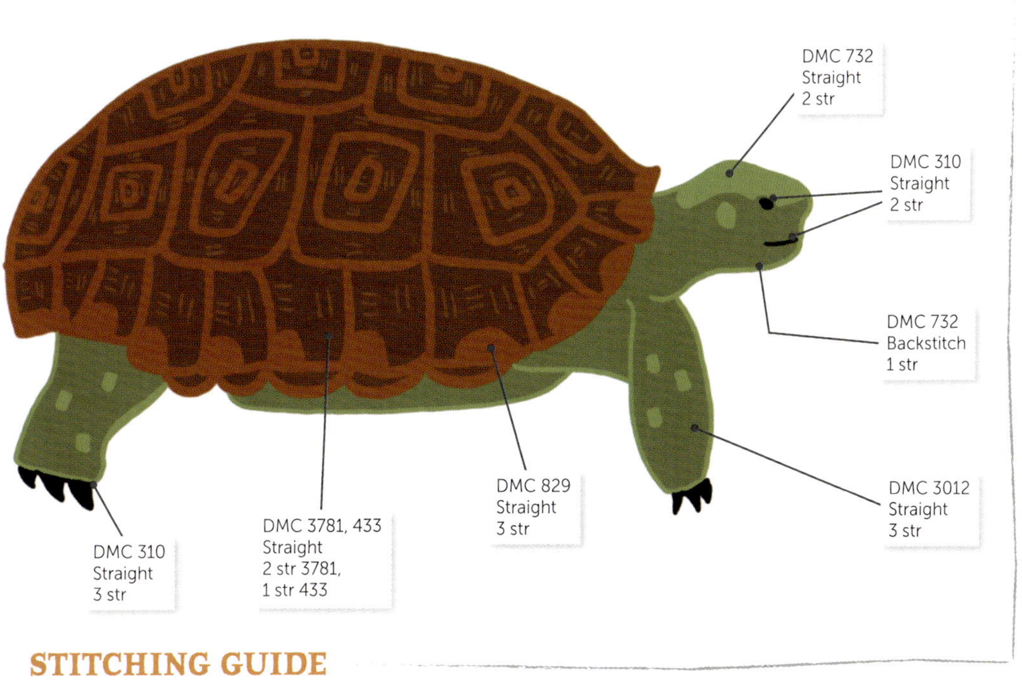
DMC 732
Straight
2 str
DMC 310
Straight
2 str
DMC 732
Backstitch
1 str
DMC 3012
Straight
3 str
DMC 829
Straight
3 str
DMC 3781, 433
Straight
2 str 3781,
1 str 433
DMC 310
Straight
3 str

STITCHING GUIDE

Stitches Used:
fur stitch, straight
Thread Colors:
DMC 3045
DMC 310
DMC 3023
DMC 3031
DMC 844
DMC 407
DMC 3865
SIZE IN THE WILD
8"

Ringtail

LATIN NAME: *Bassariscus astutus*

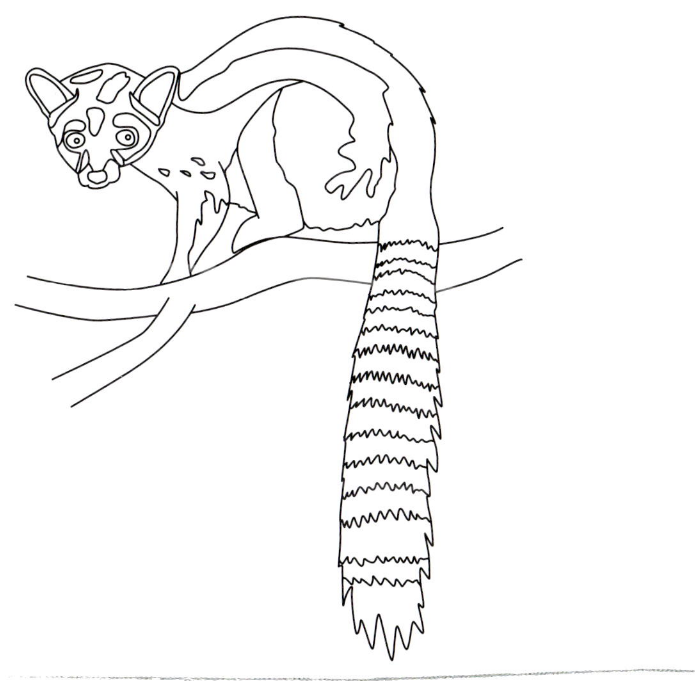

PATTERN

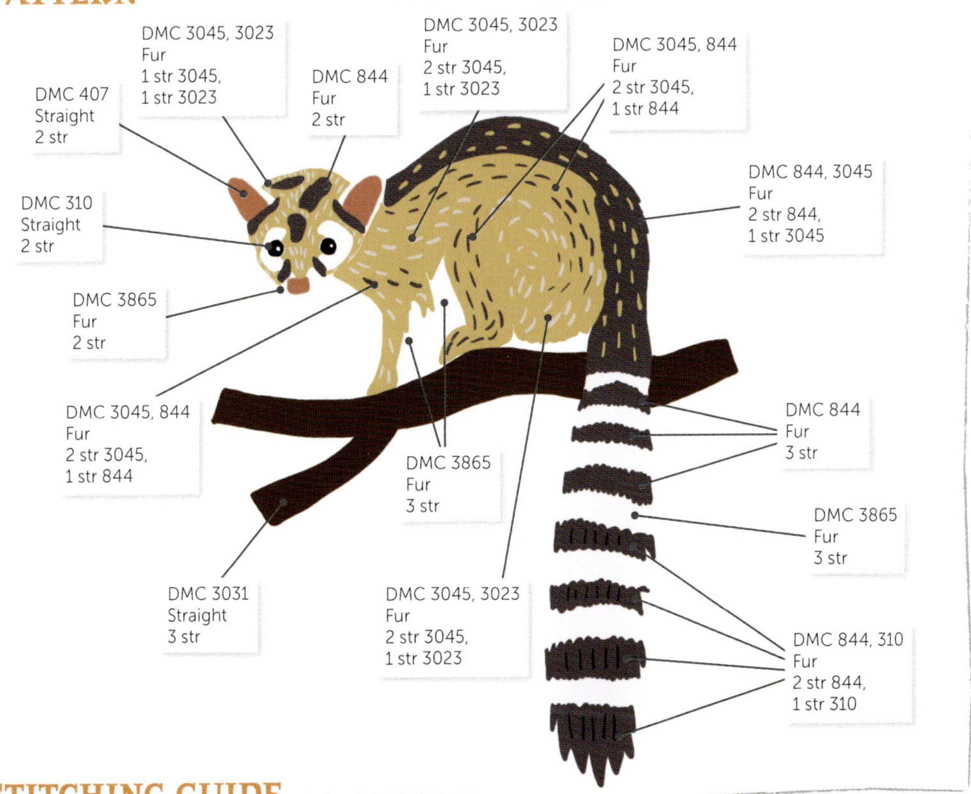
DMC 3045, 3023
Fur
1 str 3045,
1 str 3023
DMC 407
Straight
2 str
DMC 844
Fur
2 str
DMC 3045, 3023
Fur
2 str 3045,
1 str 3023
DMC 3045, 844
Fur
2 str 3045,
1 str 844
DMC 310
Straight
2 str
DMC 844, 3045
Fur
2 str 844,
1 str 3045
DMC 3865
Fur
2 str
DMC 3045, 844
Fur
2 str 3045,
1 str 844
DMC 844
Fur
3 str
DMC 3865
Fur
3 str
DMC 3865
Fur
3 str
DMC 3031
Straight
3 str
DMC 3045, 3023
Fur
2 str 3045,
1 str 3023
DMC 844, 310
Fur
2 str 844,
1 str 310

STITCHING GUIDE

Stitches Used:
backstitch, fur stitch,
straight
Thread Colors:
DMC 3809
DMC 642
DMC 3865
DMC 3799
DMC 839
DMC 407
DMC 3821
DMC 927
DMC 310
SIZE IN THE WILD
8"

Greater Roadrunner

LATIN NAME: *Geococcyx californianus*

PATTERN

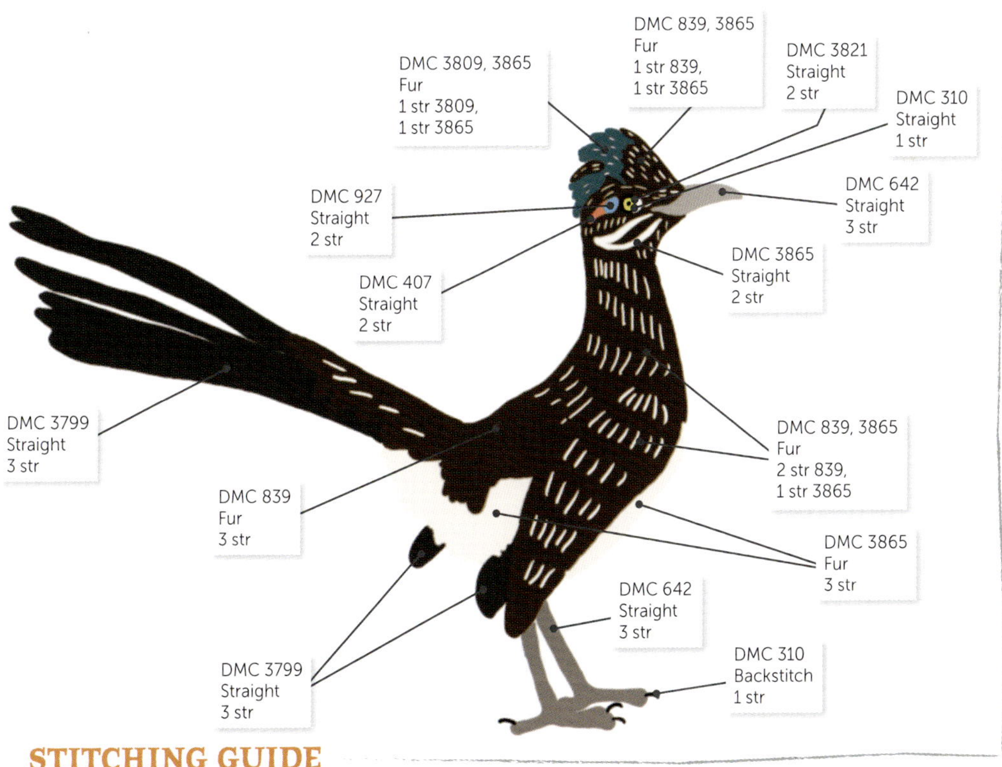

DMC 3809, 3865
Fur
1 str 3809,
1 str 3865
DMC 839, 3865
Fur
1 str 839,
1 str 3865
DMC 3821
Straight
2 str
DMC 310
Straight
1 str
DMC 642
Straight
3 str
DMC 927
Straight
2 str
DMC 3865
Straight
2 str
DMC 407
Straight
2 str
DMC 3799
Straight
3 str
DMC 839, 3865
Fur
2 str 839,
1 str 3865
DMC 839
Fur
3 str
DMC 3865
Fur
3 str
DMC 642
Straight
3 str
DMC 3799
Straight
3 str
DMC 310
Backstitch
1 str

STITCHING GUIDE

Section 2

MOUNTAIN

From the lush Smoky Mountain range to the rugged alpine terrain of the Rockies, North America has a stunning span of mountain regions that contain a diverse variety of flora and fauna. Adapting to live in high altitudes and extreme temperatures, animals such as mountain goats, boreal toads, and bighorn sheep find themselves among colorful wildflowers. Stitch one on your hiking gear to carry it with you in whatever mountain range you love the most.

Some of Earth's youngest mountains are in the Cascade Range of the US states of Washington, Oregon, and California, and began to form recently: that is, only about one million years ago.

Stitches Used:
backstitch, fur stitch, straight
Thread Colors:
DMC 3051
DMC 3866
DMC 781
DMC 934
DMC 975
DMC 844
DMC 310
SIZE IN THE WILD
8"

Boreal Toad

LATIN NAME: *Anaxyrus boreas boreas*

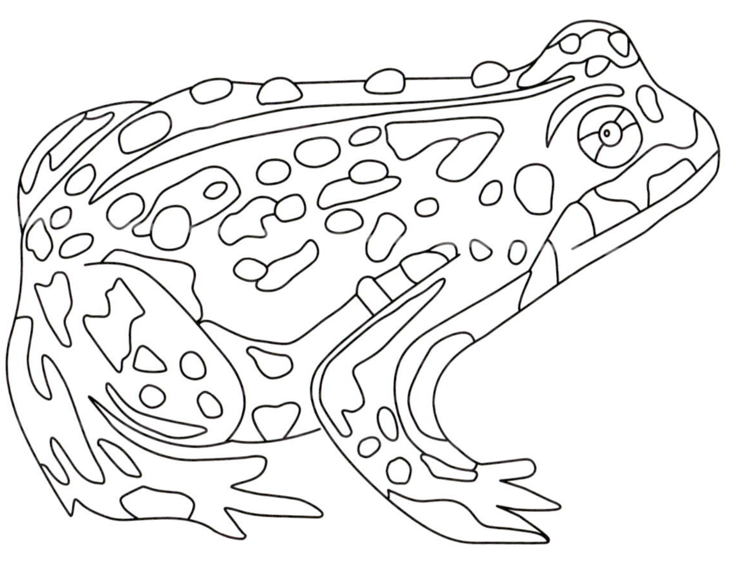

PATTERN

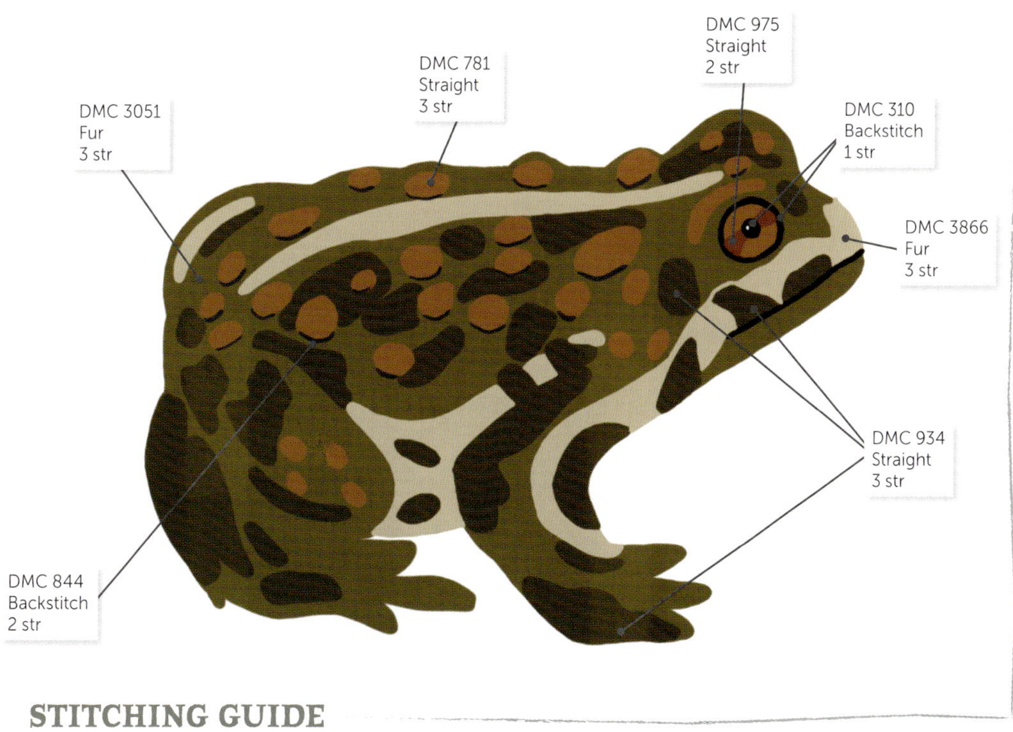
DMC 975
Straight
2 str
DMC 781
Straight
3 str
DMC 3051
Fur
3 str
DMC 310
Backstitch
1 str
DMC 3866
Fur
3 str
DMC 934
Straight
3 str
DMC 844
Backstitch
2 str

STITCHING GUIDE

Stitches Used:
fur stitch, straight
Thread Colors:
DMC ECRU
DMC 3865
DMC 310
SIZE IN THE WILD
8"

Mountain Goat

LATIN NAME: *Oreamnos americanus*

PATTERN

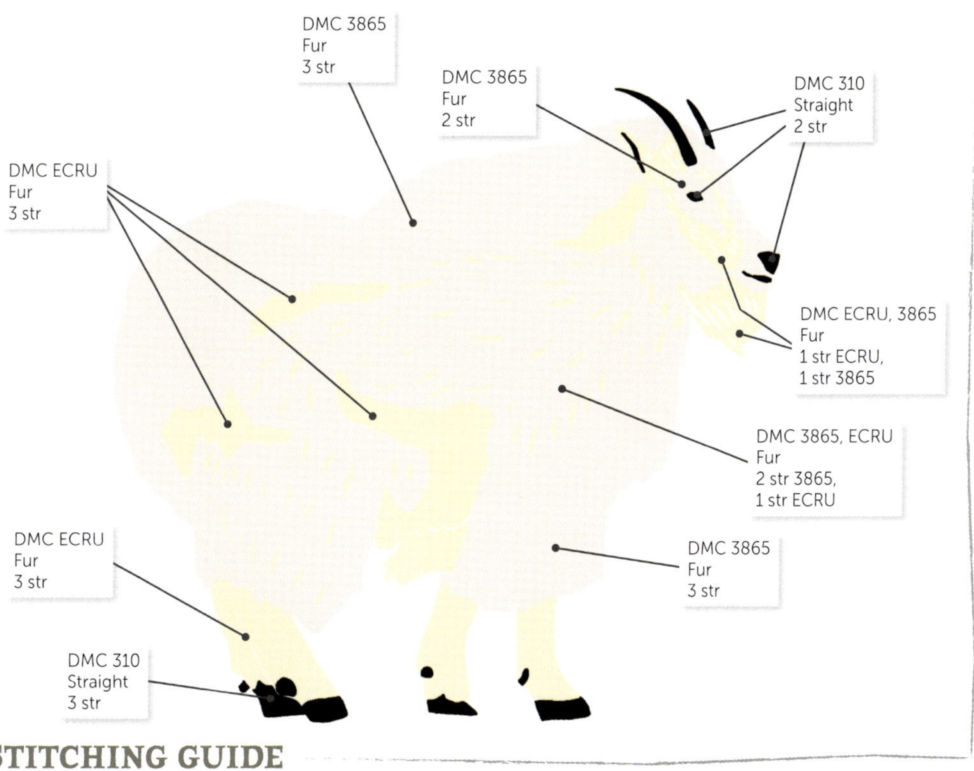
DMC 3865
Fur
3 str
DMC 3865
Fur
2 str
DMC 310
Straight
2 str
DMC ECRU
Fur
3 str
DMC ECRU, 3865
Fur
1 str ECRU,
1 str 3865
DMC 3865, ECRU
Fur
2 str 3865,
1 str ECRU
DMC ECRU
Fur
3 str
DMC 3865
Fur
3 str
DMC 310
Straight
3 str

STITCHING GUIDE

Stitches Used:
backstitch, fur stitch, straight
Thread Colors:
DMC ECRU
DMC 612
DMC 844
DMC 310
DMC 646
SIZE IN THE WILD
8"

American Pika

LATIN NAME: *Ochotona princeps*

PATTERN

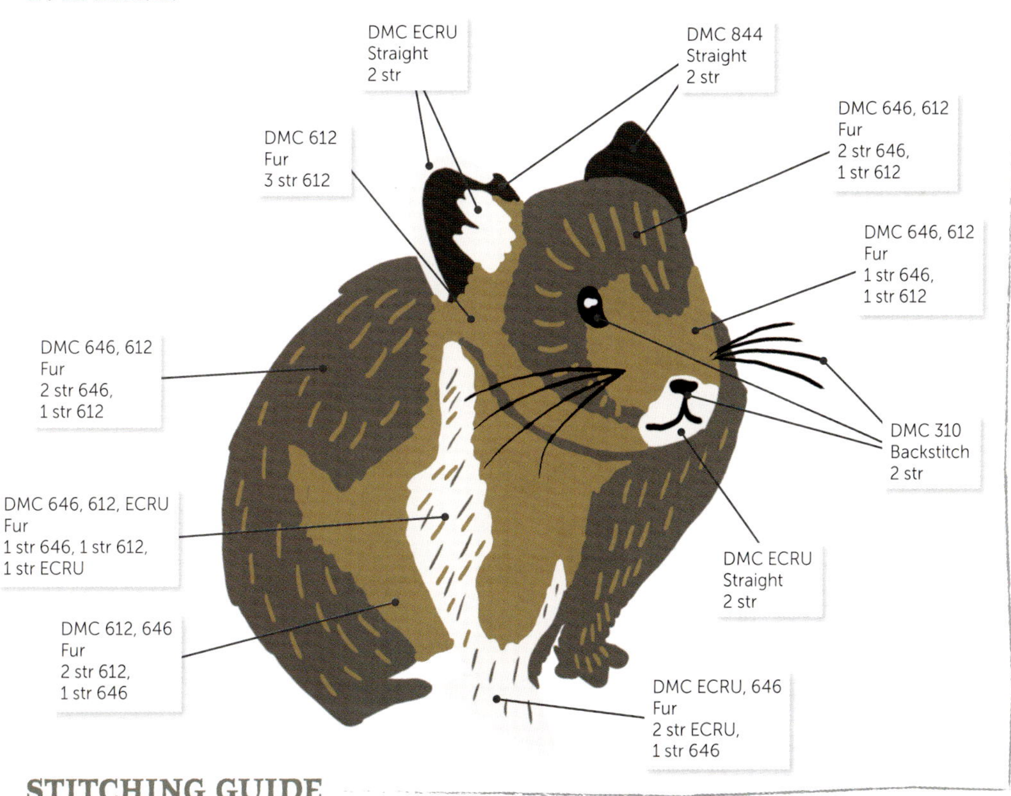

DMC ECRU
Straight
2 str
DMC 844
Straight
2 str
DMC 612
Fur
3 str 612
DMC 646, 612
Fur
2 str 646,
1 str 612
DMC 646, 612
Fur
1 str 646,
1 str 612
DMC 646, 612
Fur
2 str 646,
1 str 612
DMC 310
Backstitch
2 str
DMC 646, 612, ECRU
Fur
1 str 646, 1 str 612,
1 str ECRU
DMC ECRU
Straight
2 str
DMC 612, 646
Fur
2 str 612,
1 str 646
DMC ECRU, 646
Fur
2 str ECRU,
1 str 646

STITCHING GUIDE

Stitches Used:
backstitch, fur stitch, straight
Thread Colors:
DMC 310
DMC 3865
DMC 844
DMC 3045
DMC 167
DMC 407
DMC 3799
DMC 3821
SIZE IN THE WILD
8"

Mountain Lion

LATIN NAME: *Puma concolor*

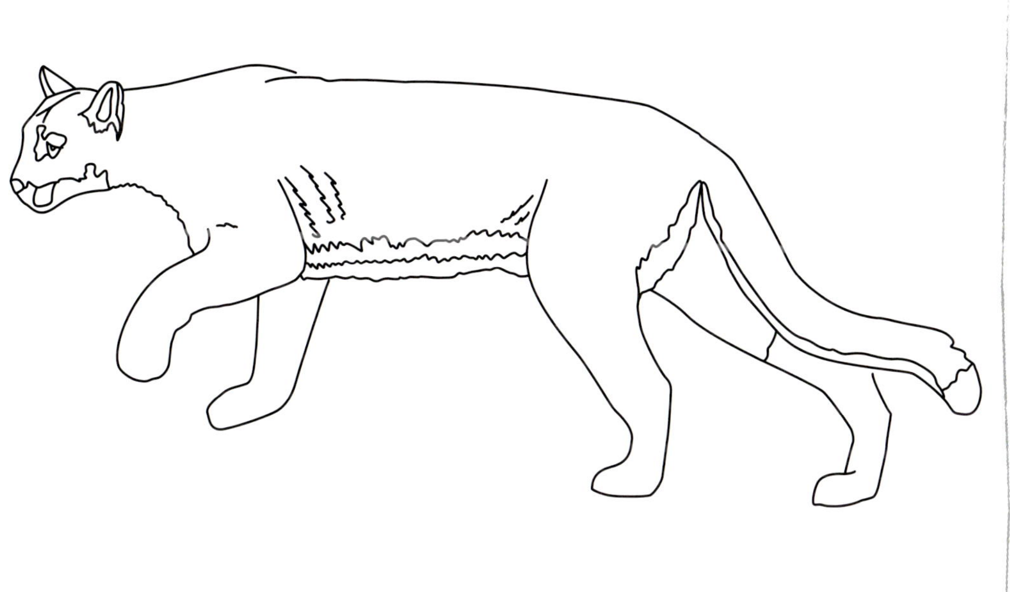

PATTERN

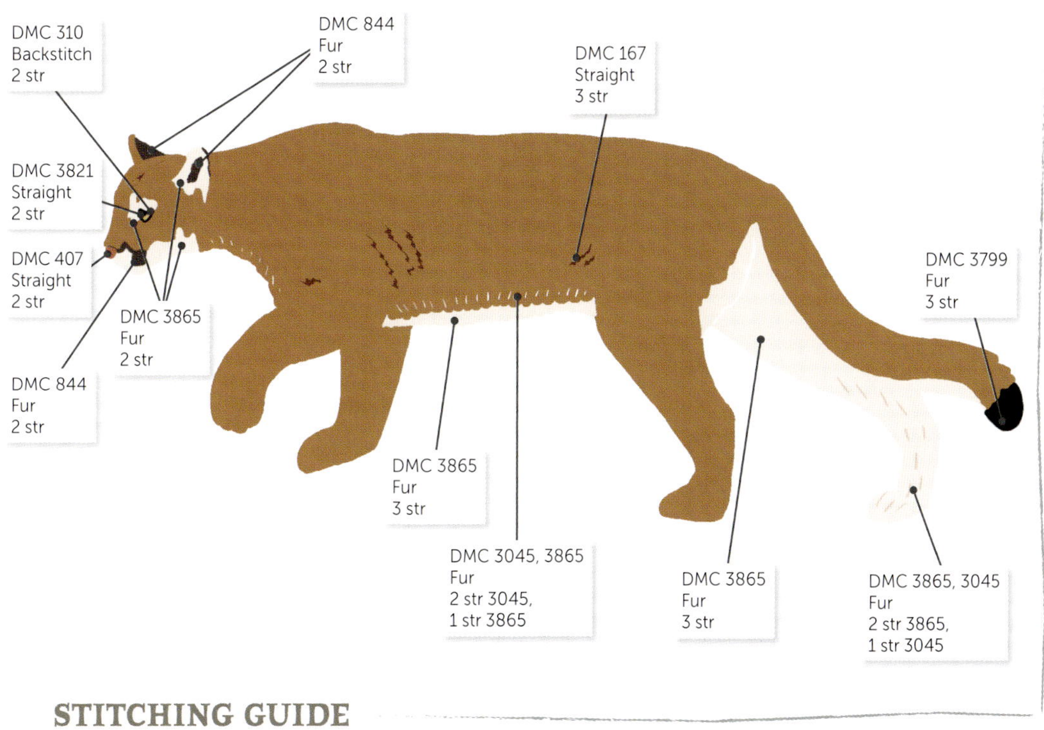
DMC 310
Backstitch
2 str
DMC 844
Fur
2 str
DMC 167
Straight
3 str
DMC 3821
Straight
2 str
DMC 407
Straight
2 str
DMC 3865
Fur
2 str
DMC 844
Fur
2 str
DMC 3799
Fur
3 str
DMC 3865
Fur
3 str
DMC 3045, 3865
Fur
2 str 3045,
1 str 3865
DMC 3865
Fur
3 str
DMC 3865, 3045
Fur
2 str 3865,
1 str 3045

STITCHING GUIDE

Stitches Used:
backstitch, fur stitch, straight
Thread Colors:
DMC ECRU
DMC 310
DMC 3790
DMC 420
DMC 839
DMC 3031
DMC 3828
DMC 829
DMC 612
DMC 3346
SIZE IN THE WILD
8"

Elk

LATIN NAME: *Cervus canadensis*

PATTERN

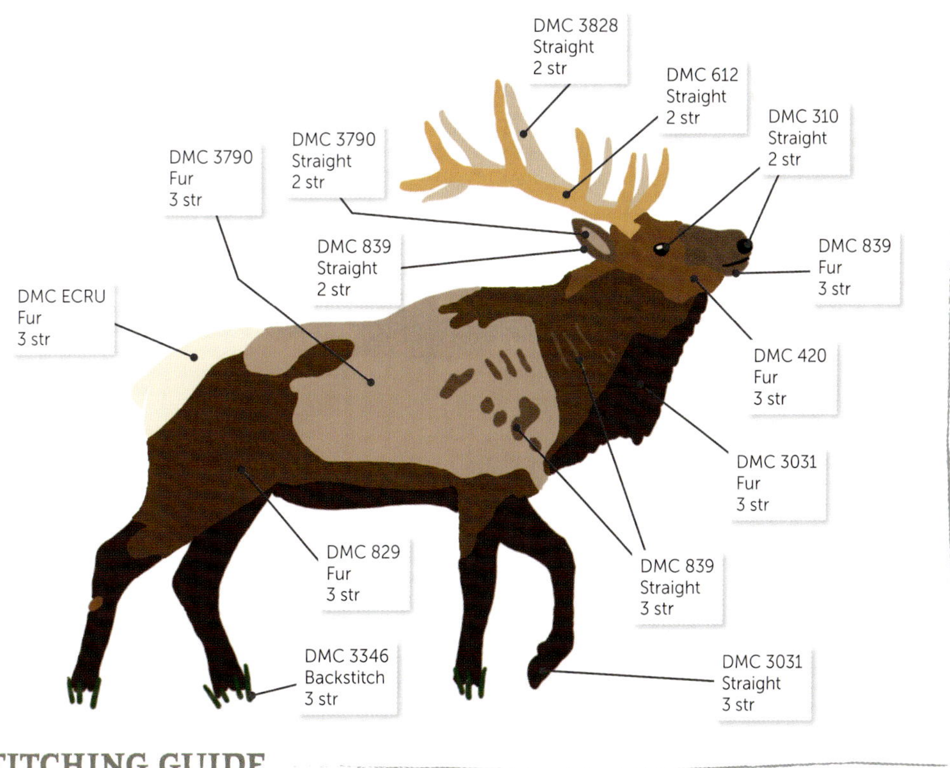

DMC 3828
Straight
2 str
DMC 612
Straight
2 str
DMC 310
Straight
2 str
DMC 3790
Straight
2 str
DMC 3790
Fur
3 str
DMC 839
Straight
2 str
DMC 839
Fur
3 str
DMC ECRU
Fur
3 str
DMC 420
Fur
3 str
DMC 3031
Fur
3 str
DMC 829
Fur
3 str
DMC 839
Straight
3 str
DMC 3346
Backstitch
3 str
DMC 3031
Straight
3 str

STITCHING GUIDE

Stitches Used:
backstitch, French knot, lazy daisy, straight

Thread Colors:

DMC ECRU	DMC 470	DMC 730
DMC 726	DMC 937	DMC 988
DMC 208	DMC 3371	DMC 553
DMC 304	DMC 725	DMC 153
DMC 3831		

SIZE IN THE WILD

8"

Wildflower Mix

(western coneflower, common yarrow, paintbrush, silvery lupine, showy fleabane)

LATIN NAMES:
Rudbeckia occidentalis, Achillea millefolium, Castilleja coccinea, Lupinus argenteus, Erigeron speciosus

PATTERN

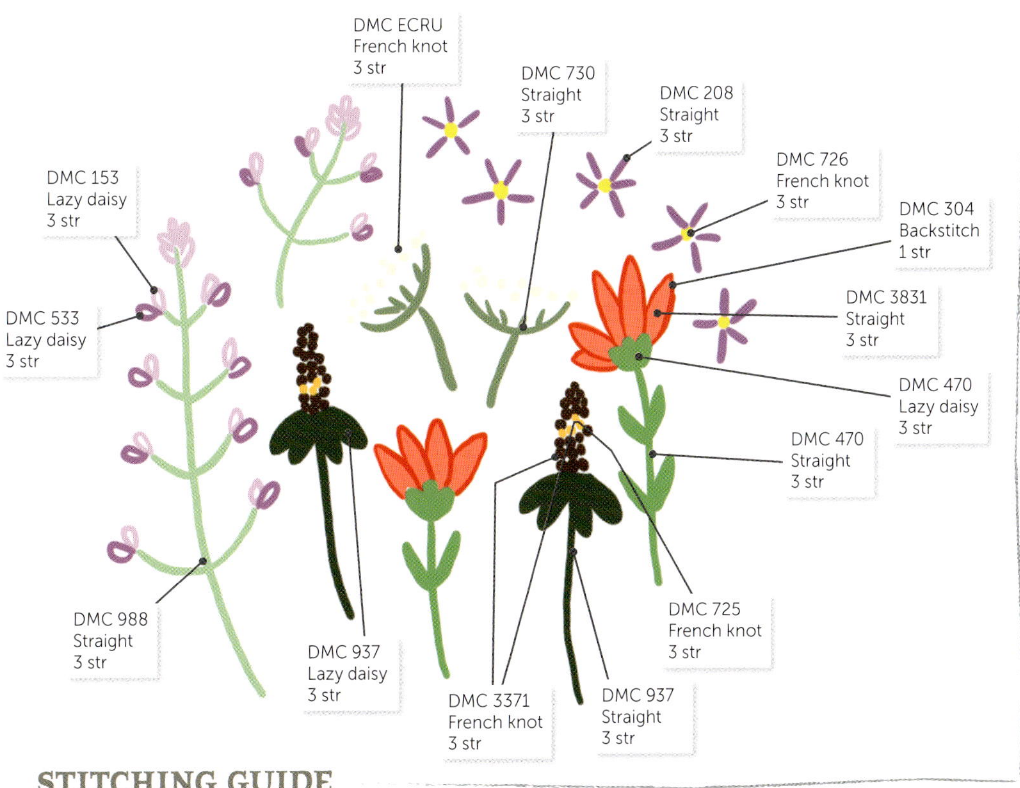

DMC ECRU
French knot
3 str
DMC 730
Straight
3 str
DMC 208
Straight
3 str
DMC 726
French knot
3 str
DMC 153
Lazy daisy
3 str
DMC 304
Backstitch
1 str
DMC 533
Lazy daisy
3 str
DMC 3831
Straight
3 str
DMC 470
Lazy daisy
3 str
DMC 470
Straight
3 str
DMC 988
Straight
3 str
DMC 725
French knot
3 str
DMC 937
Lazy daisy
3 str
DMC 3371
French knot
3 str
DMC 937
Straight
3 str

STITCHING GUIDE

Stitches Used:
fur stitch, straight
Thread Colors:
DMC 436
DMC ECRU
DMC 646
DMC 3031
DMC 3045
DMC 844
DMC 3781
DMC 310
SIZE IN THE WILD
8"

Bighorn Sheep

LATIN NAME: *Ovis canadensis*

PATTERN

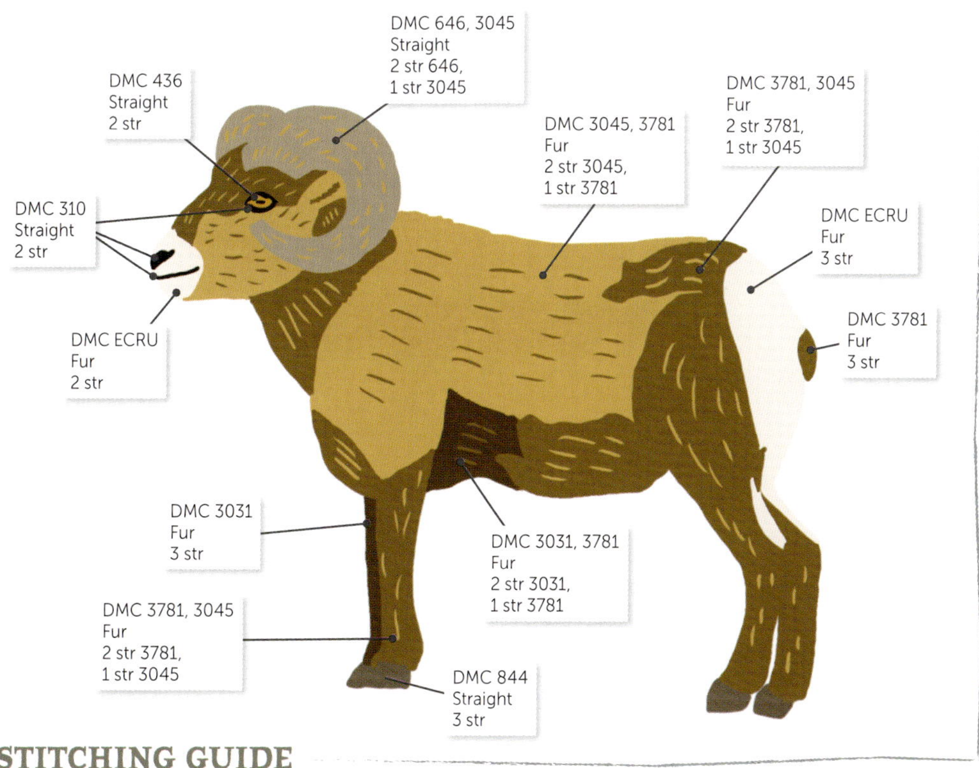

DMC 646, 3045
Straight
2 str 646,
1 str 3045
DMC 436
Straight
2 str
DMC 3045, 3781
Fur
2 str 3045,
1 str 3781
DMC 3781, 3045
Fur
2 str 3781,
1 str 3045
DMC 310
Straight
2 str
DMC ECRU
Fur
3 str
DMC ECRU
Fur
2 str
DMC 3781
Fur
3 str
DMC 3031
Fur
3 str
DMC 3031, 3781
Fur
2 str 3031,
1 str 3781
DMC 3781, 3045
Fur
2 str 3781,
1 str 3045
DMC 844
Straight
3 str

STITCHING GUIDE

Stitches Used:
fur stitch, straight
Thread Colors:
DMC 3790
DMC 310
DMC 839
DMC 356
DMC 898
DMC 3865
DMC 3371
SIZE IN THE WILD
8"

Grizzly Bear

LATIN NAME: *Ursus arctos horribilis*

PATTERN

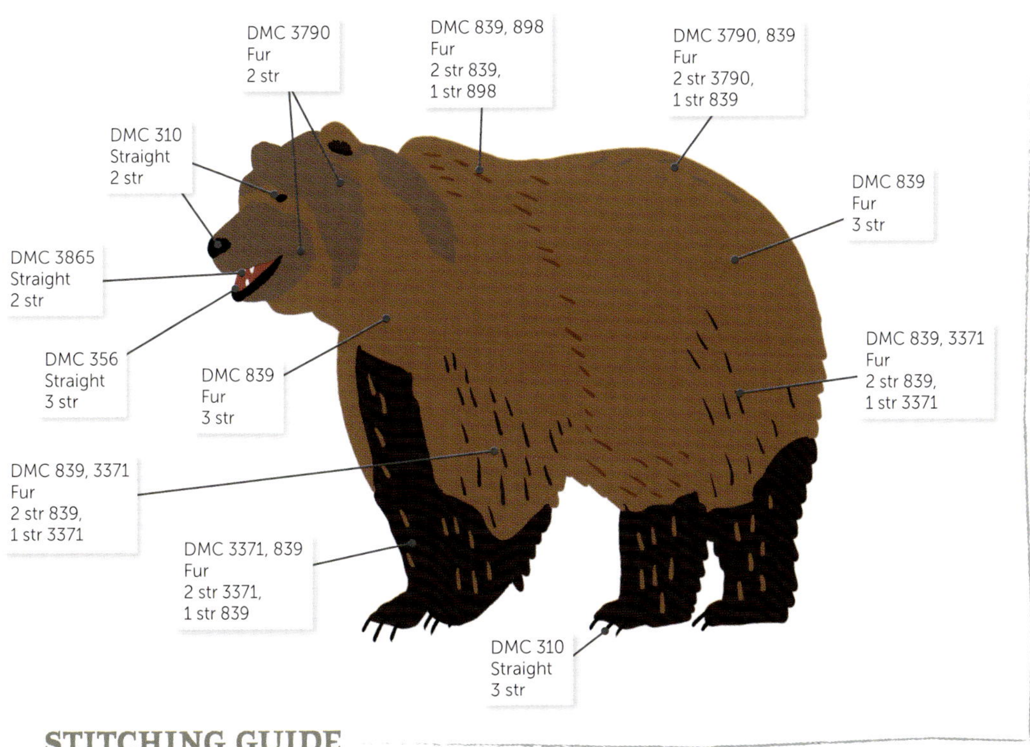
DMC 3790
Fur
2 str
DMC 839, 898
Fur
2 str 839,
1 str 898
DMC 3790, 839
Fur
2 str 3790,
1 str 839
DMC 310
Straight
2 str
DMC 839
Fur
3 str
DMC 3865
Straight
2 str
DMC 839, 3371
Fur
2 str 839,
1 str 3371
DMC 356
Straight
3 str
DMC 839
Fur
3 str
DMC 839, 3371
Fur
2 str 839,
1 str 3371
DMC 3371, 839
Fur
2 str 3371,
1 str 839
DMC 310
Straight
3 str

STITCHING GUIDE

Section 3

WATERWAYS

Lakes, rivers, and other fresh bodies of water make up the waterways ecosystem in this book. From the Great Lakes to the mighty Mississippi, the waterways ecosystem is vital to all species of wildlife. Some have adapted to rely on them nearly solely, such as fish, amphibians, and waterfowl. You'll find some of those species highlighted here, such as the osprey, American beaver, and North American river otter.

The Great Lakes–St. Lawrence River watershed is one of the largest freshwater ecosystems in the world. It contains about 84 percent of North America's fresh water.

Nikon
ACULON

Stitches Used:
backstitch, French knot, fur stitch, straight
Thread Colors:
DMC 310
DMC 3853
DMC 606
DMC 781
DMC 721
SIZE IN THE WILD
8"

Eastern Newt

LATIN NAME: *Notophthalmus viridescens*

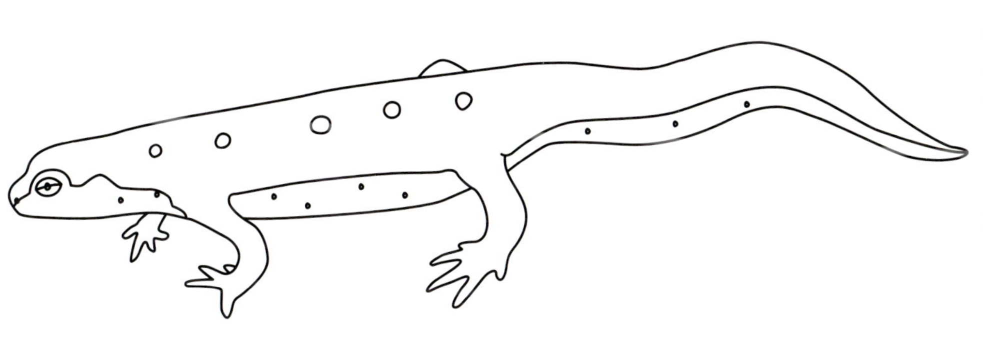

PATTERN

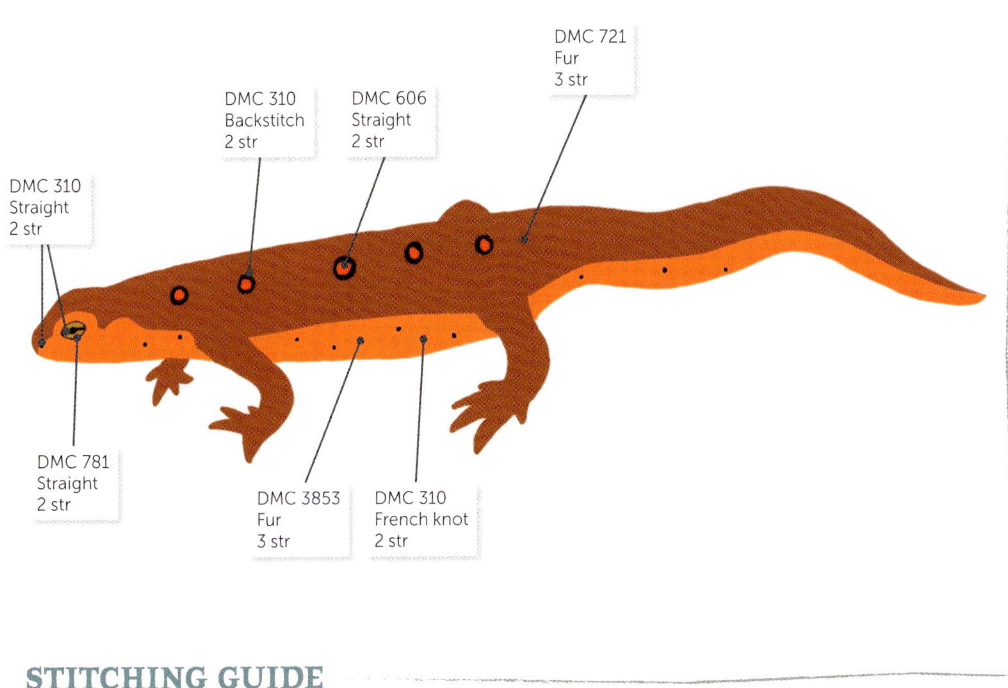
DMC 721
Fur
3 str
DMC 310
Backstitch
2 str
DMC 606
Straight
2 str
DMC 310
Straight
2 str
DMC 781
Straight
2 str
DMC 3853
Fur
3 str
DMC 310
French knot
2 str

STITCHING GUIDE

Stitches Used:
straight
Thread Colors:
DMC 3781
DMC 725
DMC 3371
DMC 844
DMC 3865
DMC ECRU
DMC 310
SIZE IN THE WILD
8"

Osprey

LATIN NAME: *Pandion haliaetus*

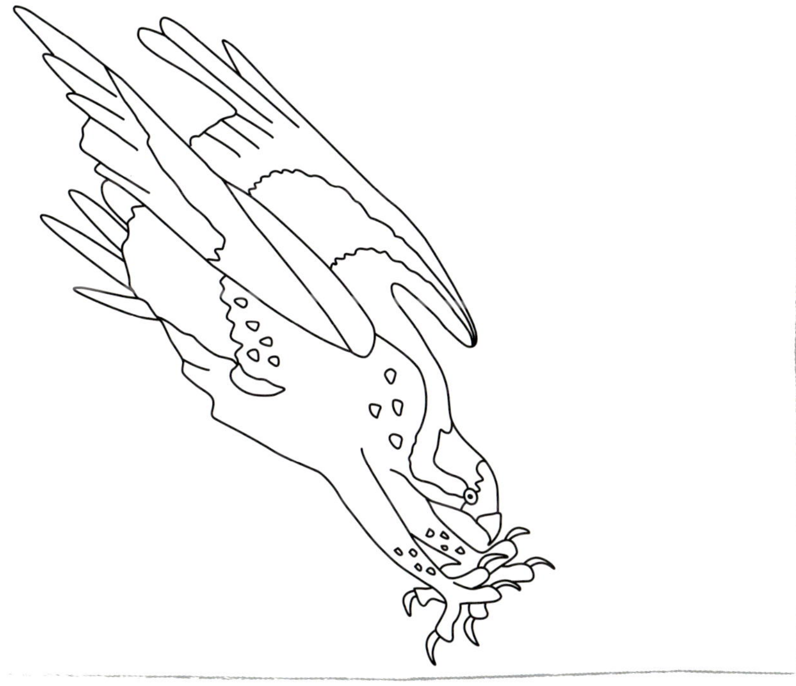

PATTERN

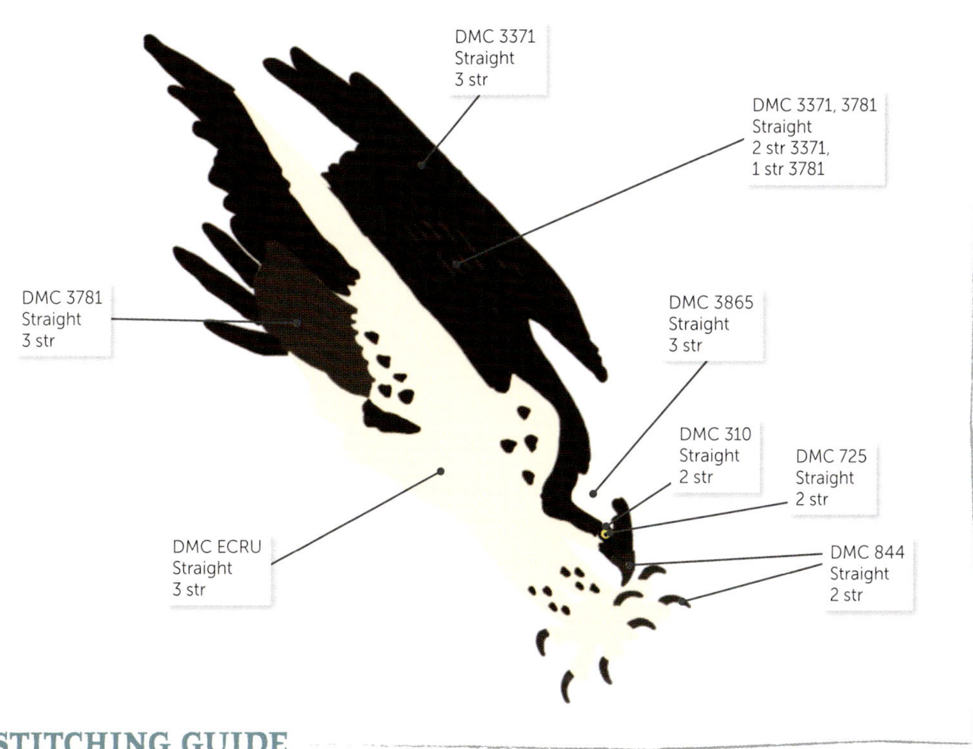

DMC 3371
Straight
3 str
DMC 3371, 3781
Straight
2 str 3371,
1 str 3781
DMC 3781
Straight
3 str
DMC 3865
Straight
3 str
DMC 310
Straight
2 str
DMC 725
Straight
2 str
DMC ECRU
Straight
3 str
DMC 844
Straight
2 str

STITCHING GUIDE

Stitches Used:
backstitch, straight
Thread Colors:
DMC 844
DMC 3765
DMC 3865
DMC 3809
DMC 310
DMC 924
DMC 22
SIZE IN THE WILD
8"

Common Loon

LATIN NAME: *Gavia immer*

PATTERN

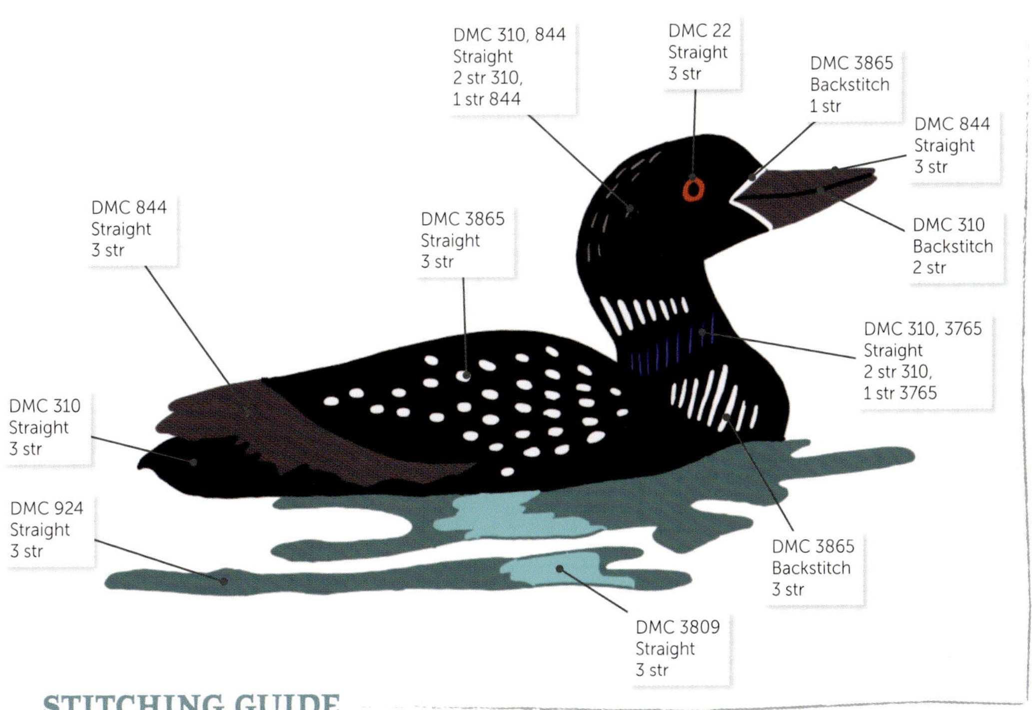
DMC 310, 844
Straight
2 str 310,
1 str 844
DMC 22
Straight
3 str
DMC 3865
Backstitch
1 str
DMC 844
Straight
3 str
DMC 310
Backstitch
2 str
DMC 844
Straight
3 str
DMC 3865
Straight
3 str
DMC 310, 3765
Straight
2 str 310,
1 str 3765
DMC 310
Straight
3 str
DMC 924
Straight
3 str
DMC 3865
Backstitch
3 str
DMC 3809
Straight
3 str

STITCHING GUIDE

Stitches Used:
fur stitch, straight
Thread Colors:
DMC 310
DMC 3781
DMC 844
DMC 3371
DMC 829
DMC 781
SIZE IN THE WILD
8"

American Beaver

LATIN NAME: *Castor canadensis*

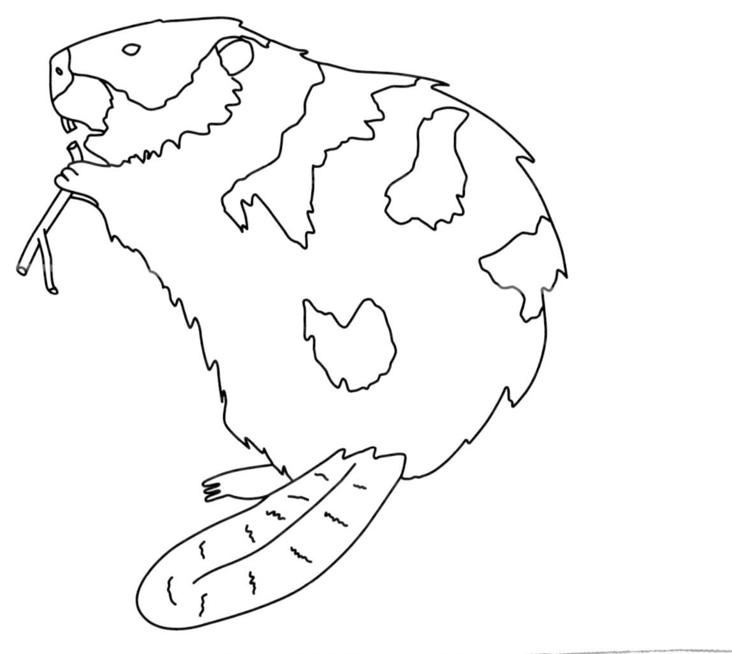

PATTERN

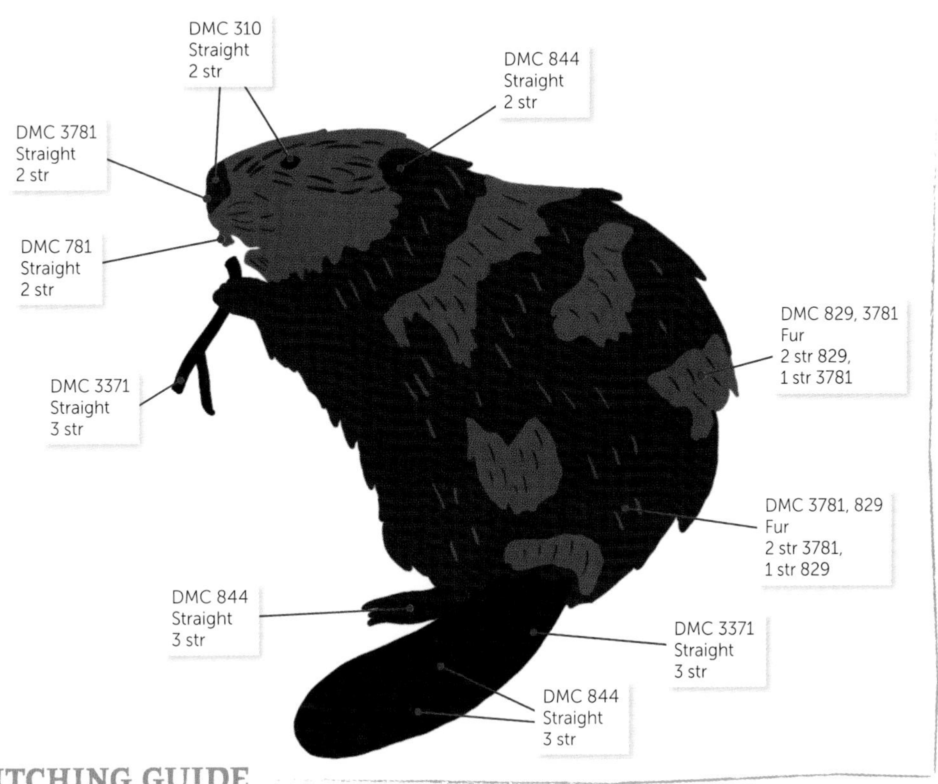
DMC 310
Straight
2 str
DMC 844
Straight
2 str
DMC 3781
Straight
2 str
DMC 781
Straight
2 str
DMC 3371
Straight
3 str
DMC 829, 3781
Fur
2 str 829,
1 str 3781
DMC 3781, 829
Fur
2 str 3781,
1 str 829
DMC 844
Straight
3 str
DMC 3371
Straight
3 str
DMC 844
Straight
3 str

STITCHING GUIDE

Stitches Used:
backstitch, fur stitch, straight
Thread Colors:
DMC 645
DMC 3765
DMC 869
DMC 3799
DMC 898
DMC 310
DMC 938
DMC 844
SIZE IN THE WILD
8"

North American River Otter

LATIN NAME: *Lontra canadensis*

PATTERN

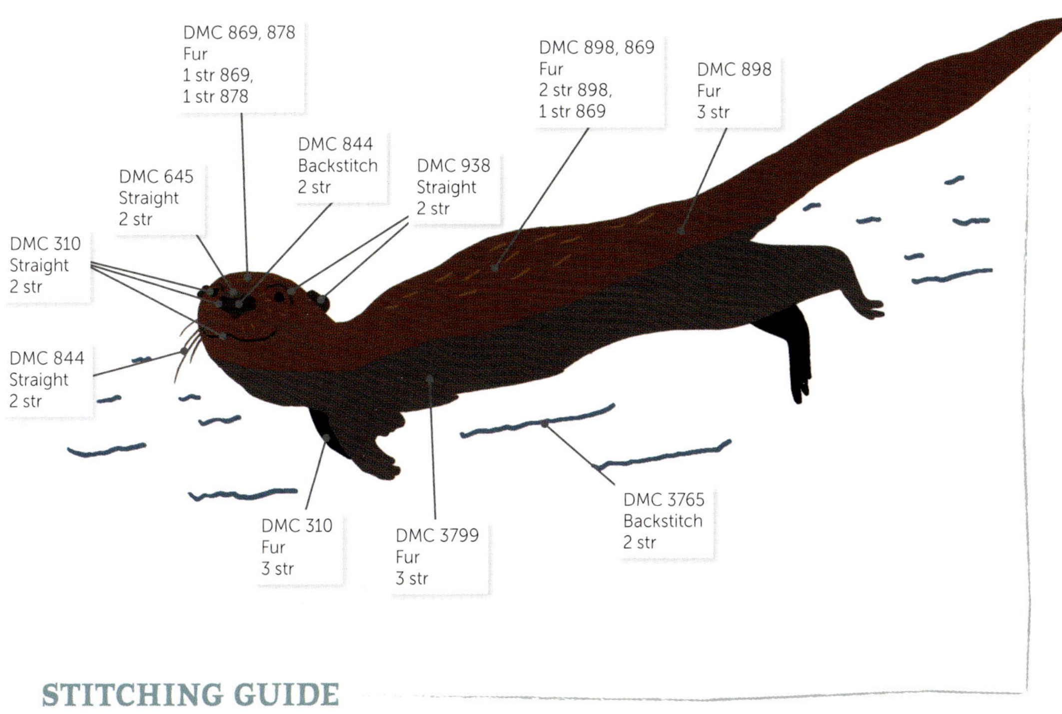
DMC 869, 878
Fur
1 str 869,
1 str 878
DMC 898, 869
Fur
2 str 898,
1 str 869
DMC 898
Fur
3 str
DMC 844
Backstitch
2 str
DMC 645
Straight
2 str
DMC 938
Straight
2 str
DMC 310
Straight
2 str
DMC 844
Straight
2 str
DMC 310
Fur
3 str
DMC 3799
Fur
3 str
DMC 3765
Backstitch
2 str

STITCHING GUIDE

Stitches Used:
backstitch, fur stitch, straight
Thread Colors:
DMC 3866
DMC 927
DMC 937
DMC 350
DMC 22
DMC 310
SIZE IN THE WILD
8"

Sockeye Salmon

LATIN NAME: *Oncorhynchus nerka*

PATTERN

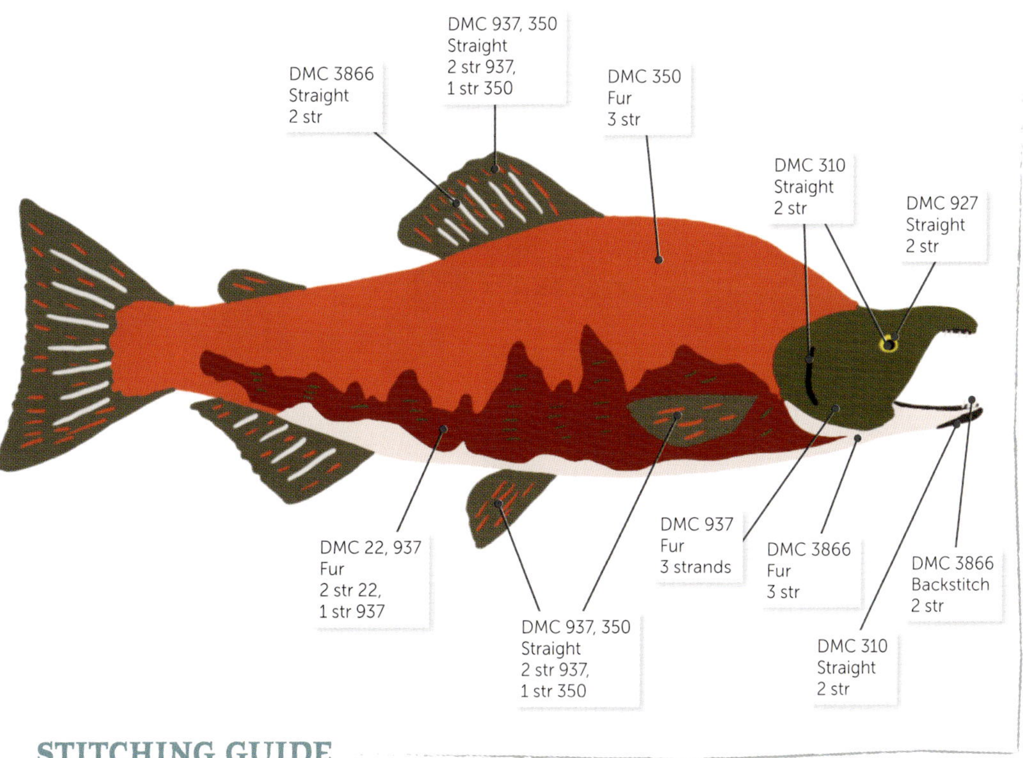
DMC 3866
Straight
2 str
DMC 937, 350
Straight
2 str 937,
1 str 350
DMC 350
Fur
3 str
DMC 310
Straight
2 str
DMC 927
Straight
2 str
DMC 22, 937
Fur
2 str 22,
1 str 937
DMC 937, 350
Straight
2 str 937,
1 str 350
DMC 937
Fur
3 strands
DMC 3866
Fur
3 str
DMC 3866
Backstitch
2 str
DMC 310
Straight
2 str

STITCHING GUIDE

Stitches Used:
backstitch, straight
Thread Colors:
DMC 646
DMC 3799
DMC 310
DMC 927
DMC 3799
SIZE IN THE WILD
8"

American Alligator

LATIN NAME: *Alligator mississippiensis*

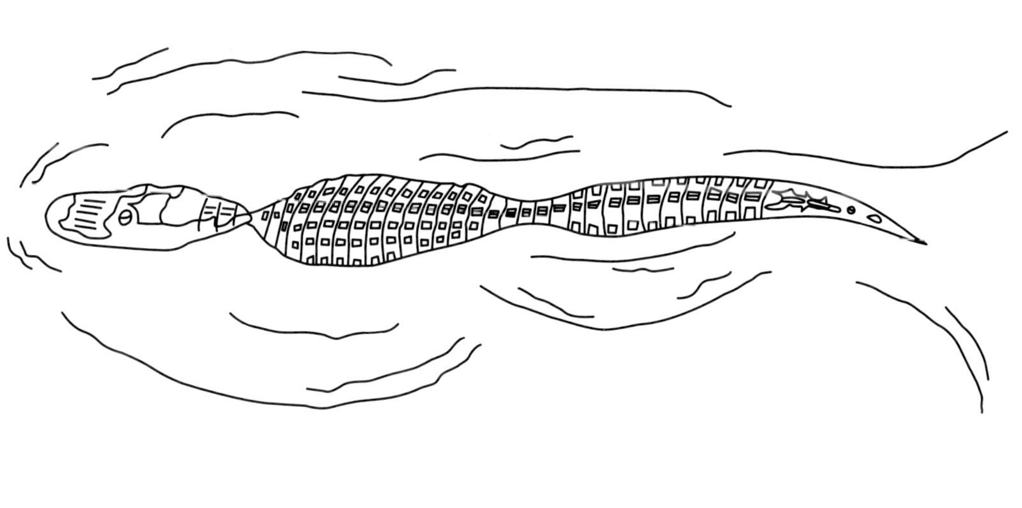

PATTERN

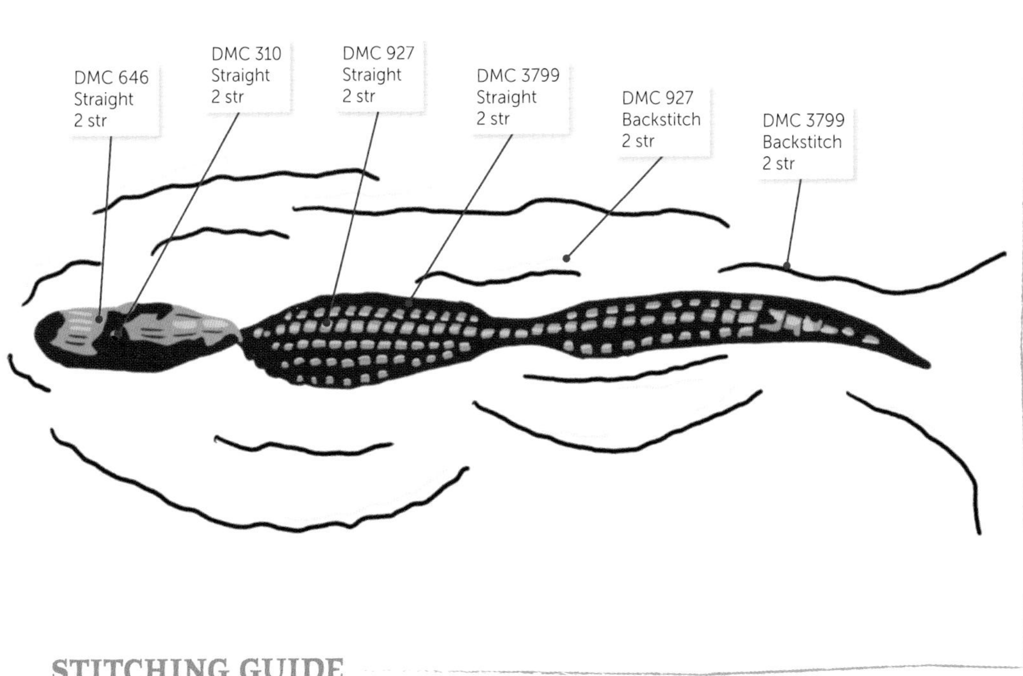
DMC 646
Straight
2 str
DMC 310
Straight
2 str
DMC 927
Straight
2 str
DMC 3799
Straight
2 str
DMC 927
Backstitch
2 str
DMC 3799
Backstitch
2 str

STITCHING GUIDE

Section 4

FOREST

From the deciduous forests of the eastern US, to the boreal forests of Canada, to the coniferous giants of the Pacific Northwest, forests are where some of our most iconic species live, such as bears, wolves, and moose. Find their patterns in this chapter, among some less celebrated but still incredibly important species such as the little brown bat.

North America's portion of the boreal forest spans Alaska and Canada, and at about 1.2 billion acres it's considered the largest intact forest left on Earth.

Stitches Used:
backstitch, fur stitch, straight
Thread Colors:
DMC 839
DMC 310
DMC 435
DMC 938
DMC 437
DMC 938
DMC 844
SIZE IN THE WILD
8"

Moose

LATIN NAME: *Alces alces*

PATTERN

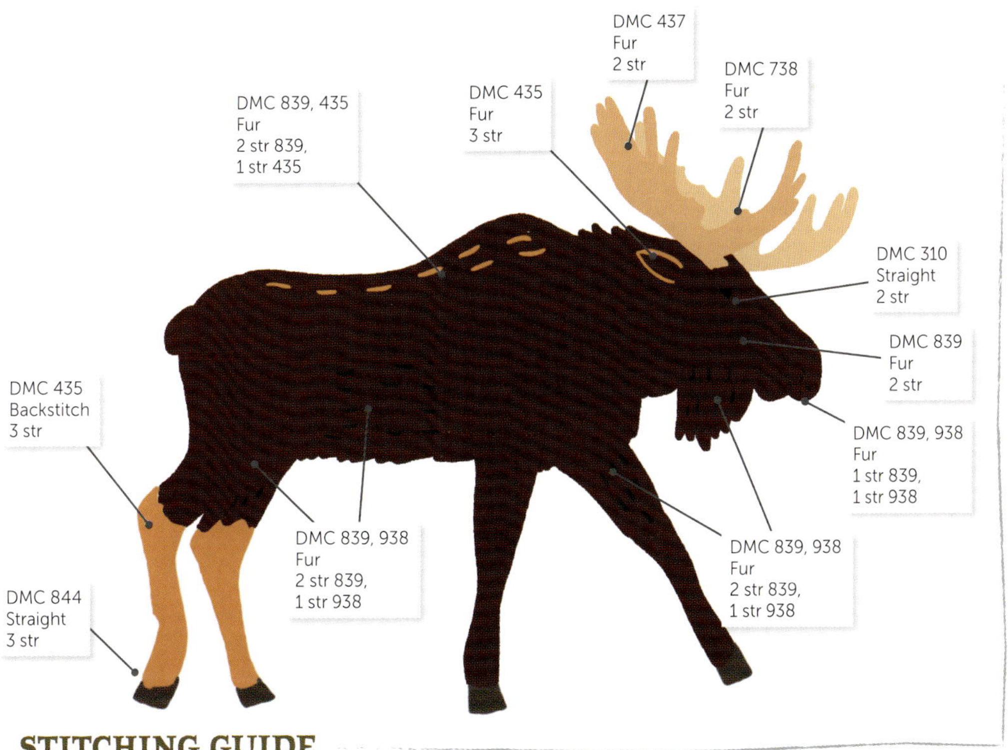
DMC 437
Fur
2 str
DMC 738
Fur
2 str
DMC 839, 435
Fur
2 str 839,
1 str 435
DMC 435
Fur
3 str
DMC 310
Straight
2 str
DMC 839
Fur
2 str
DMC 839, 938
Fur
1 str 839,
1 str 938
DMC 435
Backstitch
3 str
DMC 839, 938
Fur
2 str 839,
1 str 938
DMC 839, 938
Fur
2 str 839,
1 str 938
DMC 844
Straight
3 str

STITCHING GUIDE

Stitches Used:
French knot, fur stitch, straight
Thread Colors:
DMC 310
DMC 729
DMC 3799
DMC 3865
DMC 646
SIZE IN THE WILD
8"

Black Bear

LATIN NAME: *Ursus americanus*

PATTERN

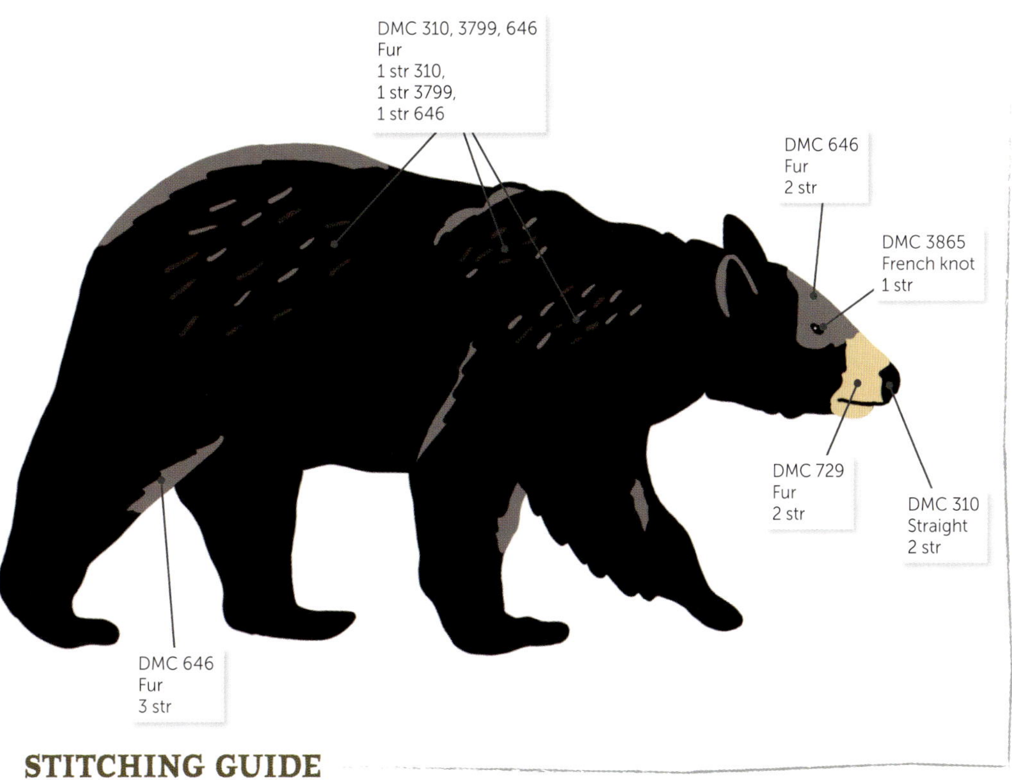
DMC 310, 3799, 646
Fur
1 str 310,
1 str 3799,
1 str 646
DMC 646
Fur
2 str
DMC 3865
French knot
1 str
DMC 729
Fur
2 str
DMC 310
Straight
2 str
DMC 646
Fur
3 str

STITCHING GUIDE

Stitches Used:
fur stitch, straight
Thread Colors:
DMC 3799
DMC ECRU
DMC 310
DMC 645
DMC 3045
SIZE IN THE WILD
8"

Gray Wolf

LATIN NAME: *Canis lupus*

PATTERN

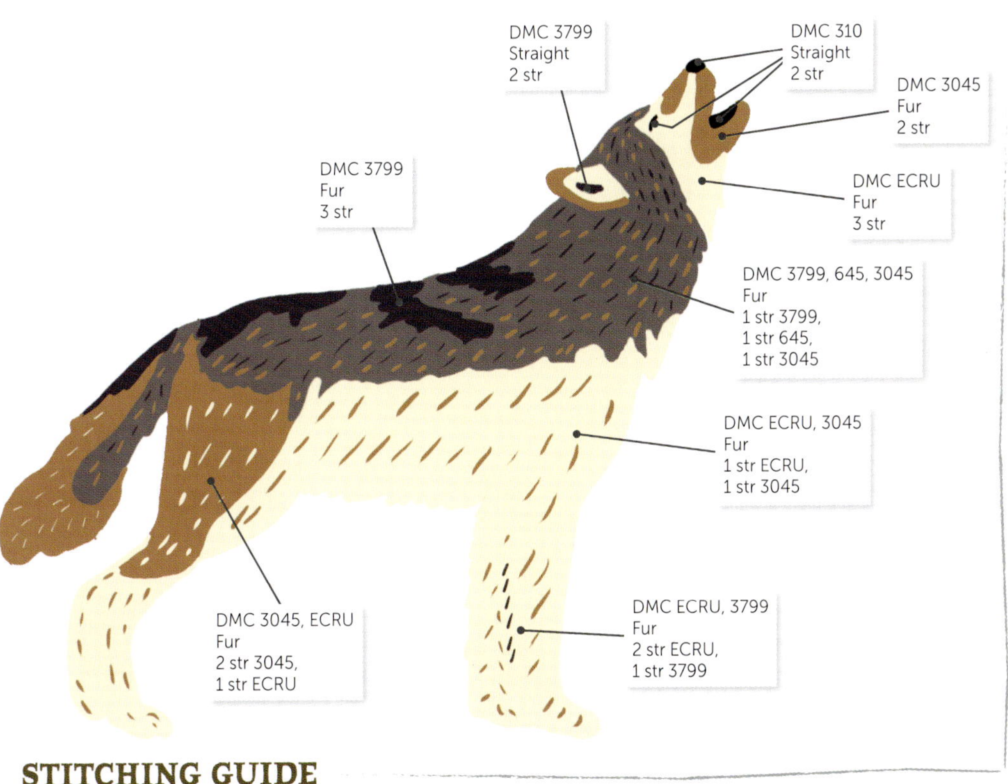
DMC 3799
Straight
2 str
DMC 310
Straight
2 str
DMC 3045
Fur
2 str
DMC 3799
Fur
3 str
DMC ECRU
Fur
3 str
DMC 3799, 645, 3045
Fur
1 str 3799,
1 str 645,
1 str 3045
DMC ECRU, 3045
Fur
1 str ECRU,
1 str 3045
DMC 3045, ECRU
Fur
2 str 3045,
1 str ECRU
DMC ECRU, 3799
Fur
2 str ECRU,
1 str 3799

STITCHING GUIDE

Stitches Used:
French knot, fur stitch, straight
Thread Colors:
DMC 3865
DMC 938
DMC 838
DMC 310
DMC 3781
DMC 844
DMC 3866
SIZE IN THE WILD
8"

Barred Owl

LATIN NAME: *Strix varia*

PATTERN

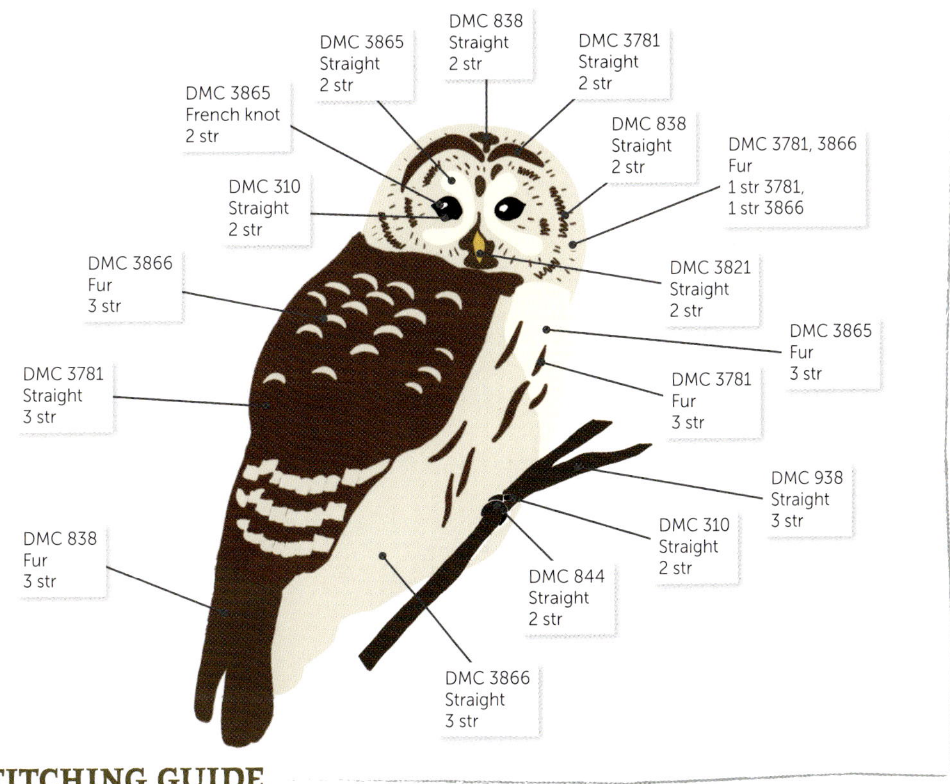
DMC 3865
Straight
2 str
DMC 838
Straight
2 str
DMC 3781
Straight
2 str
DMC 3865
French knot
2 str
DMC 838
Straight
2 str
DMC 3781, 3866
Fur
1 str 3781,
1 str 3866
DMC 310
Straight
2 str
DMC 3866
Fur
3 str
DMC 3821
Straight
2 str
DMC 3865
Fur
3 str
DMC 3781
Straight
3 str
DMC 3781
Fur
3 str
DMC 938
Straight
3 str
DMC 310
Straight
2 str
DMC 838
Fur
3 str
DMC 844
Straight
2 str
DMC 3866
Straight
3 str

STITCHING GUIDE

Stitches Used:
fur stitch, straight
Thread Colors:
DMC 839
DMC 3799
DMC 3865
DMC 646
DMC 22
DMC 167
DMC 310
DMC 3862
SIZE IN THE WILD
8"

Little Brown Bat

LATIN NAME: *Myotis lucifugus*

PATTERN

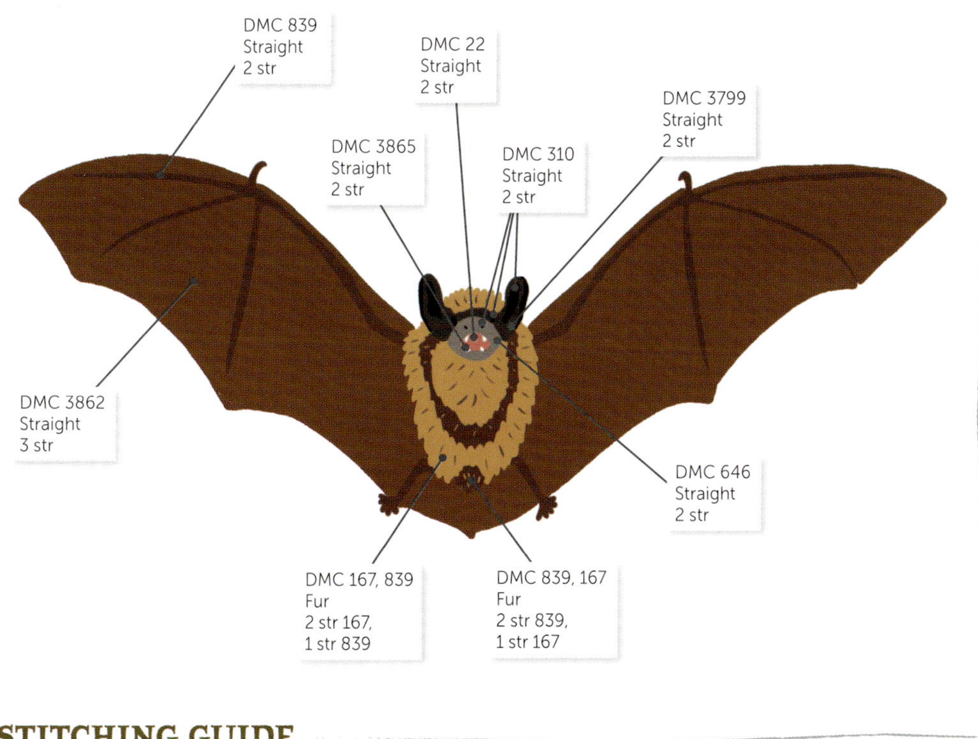
DMC 839
Straight
2 str
DMC 22
Straight
2 str
DMC 3799
Straight
2 str
DMC 3865
Straight
2 str
DMC 310
Straight
2 str
DMC 3862
Straight
3 str
DMC 646
Straight
2 str
DMC 167, 839
Fur
2 str 167,
1 str 839
DMC 839, 167
Fur
2 str 839,
1 str 167

STITCHING GUIDE

Stitches Used:
backstitch, fur stitch, straight
Thread Colors:
DMC 3031
DMC 310
DMC 3781
DMC 3865
DMC 844
DMC 666
SIZE IN THE WILD
8"

Downy Woodpecker

LATIN NAME: *Picoides pubescens*

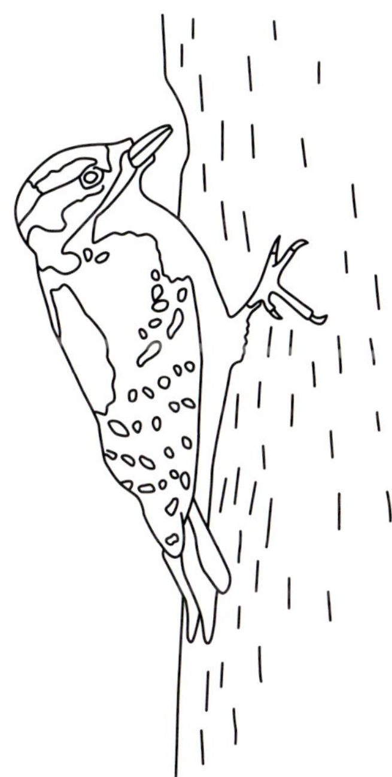

PATTERN

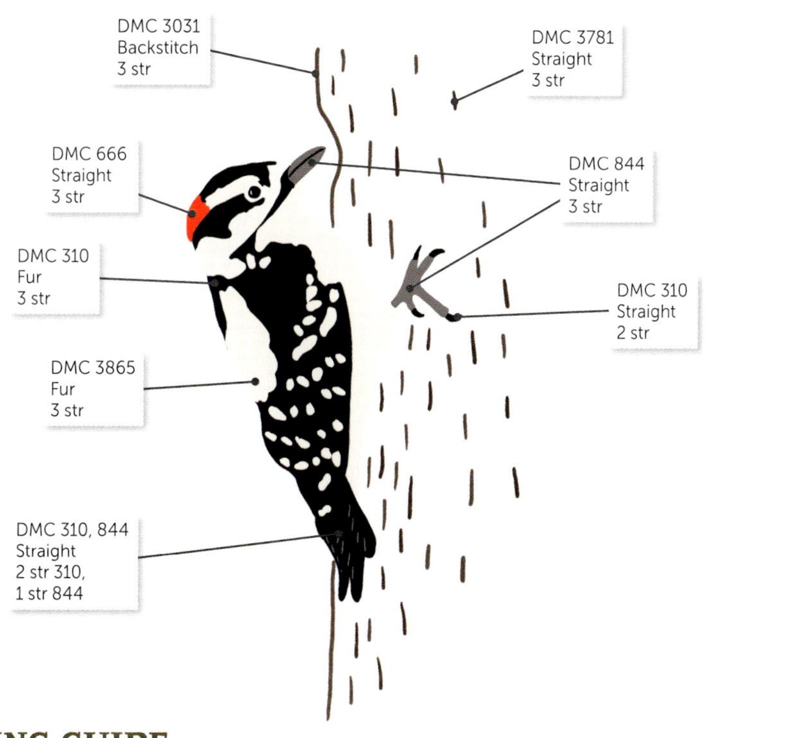
DMC 3031
Backstitch
3 str
DMC 3781
Straight
3 str
DMC 666
Straight
3 str
DMC 844
Straight
3 str
DMC 310
Fur
3 str
DMC 310
Straight
2 str
DMC 3865
Fur
3 str
DMC 310, 844
Straight
2 str 310,
1 str 844

STITCHING GUIDE

Stitches Used:
backstitch, straight
Thread Colors:
DMC 420
DMC 904
SIZE IN THE WILD
8"

Spruce Twigs

LATIN NAME: *Picea glauca*

PATTERN

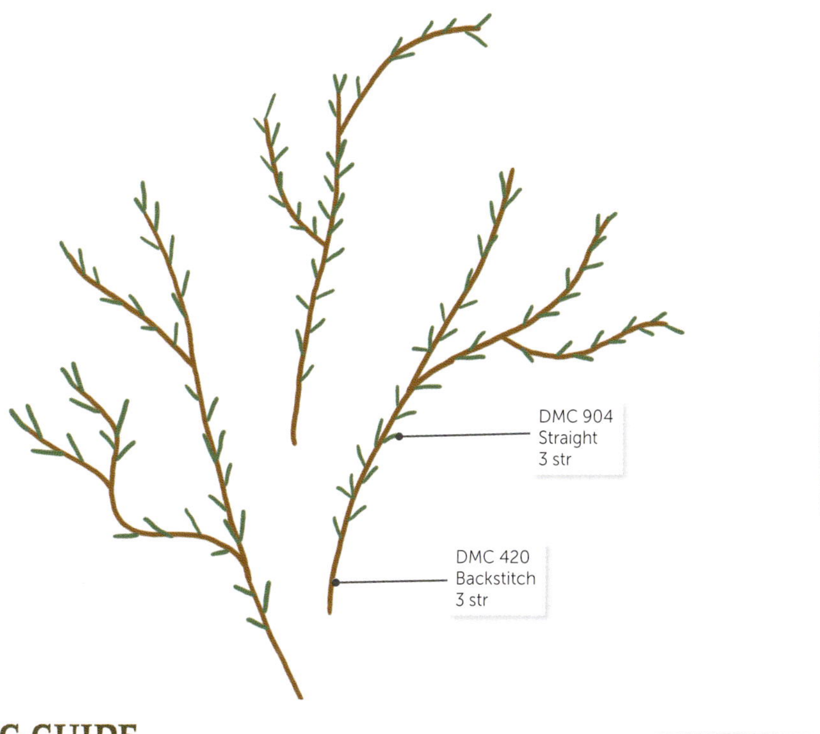
DMC 904
Straight
3 str
DMC 420
Backstitch
3 str

STITCHING GUIDE

Chapter 5

OCEAN

The ocean ecosystem across North America is expansive, including both Atlantic and Pacific Oceans, gulfs, coastal wetlands, and tidepools; they all offer vibrant biodiversity. In this chapter you'll find some of the amazing species that rely on marine habitats, such as the tufted puffin, orca, manatee, and sea turtle.

The National Marine Sanctuaries, a network of underwater parks, cover more than 620,000 square miles of marine and Great Lakes waters. Lake Ontario, the Florida Keys, and American Samoa are a few of these places.

Stitches Used:
fur stitch, straight
Thread Colors:
DMC 844
DMC 310
DMC 3865
SIZE IN THE WILD
8"

Orca

LATIN NAME: *Orcinus orca*

PATTERN

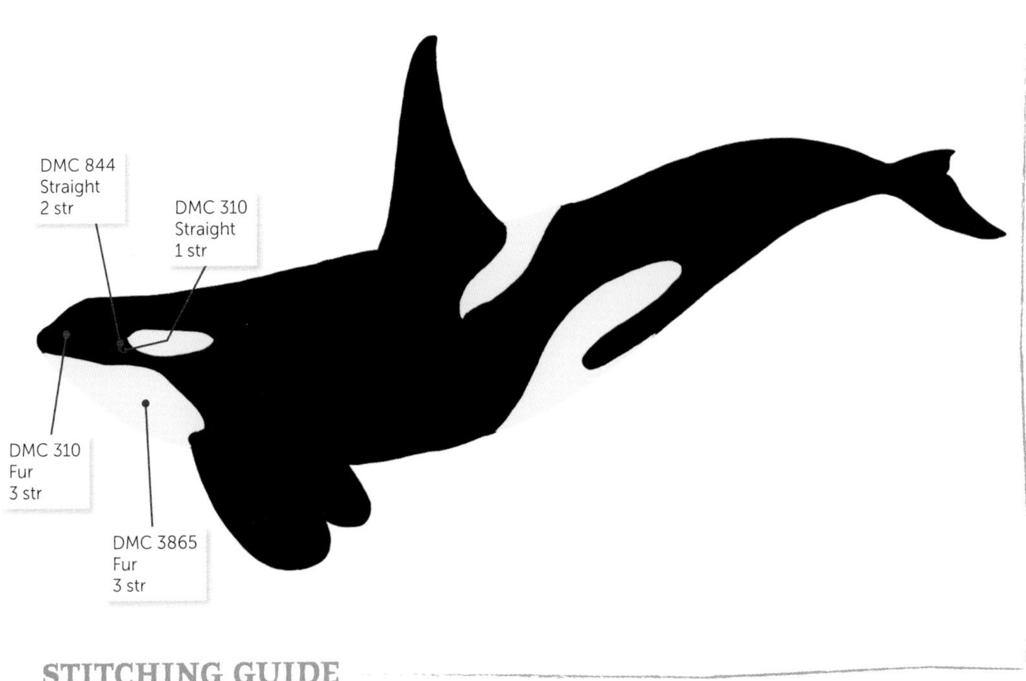
DMC 844
Straight
2 str
DMC 310
Straight
1 str
DMC 310
Fur
3 str
DMC 3865
Fur
3 str

STITCHING GUIDE

Stitches Used:
backstitch, French knot, fur stitch
Thread Colors:
DMC 422
DMC 3826
DMC 169
DMC 3865
DMC 924
DMC 3740
DMC 844
SIZE IN THE WILD
8"

Ochre Sea Star

LATIN NAME: *Pisaster ochraceus*

PATTERN

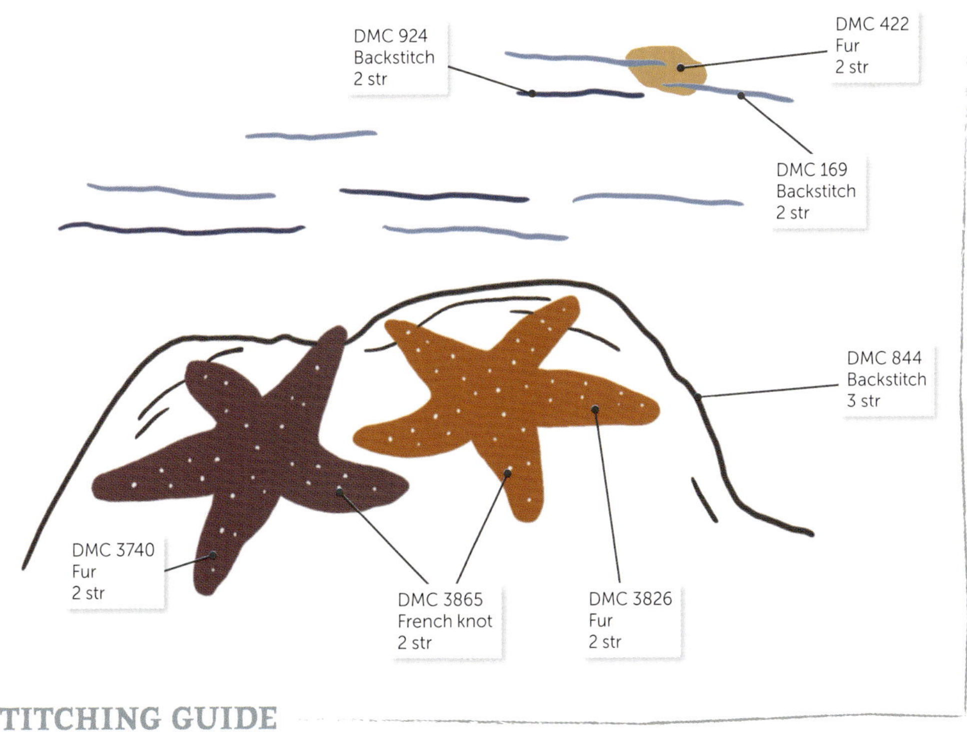
DMC 924
Backstitch
2 str
DMC 422
Fur
2 str
DMC 169
Backstitch
2 str
DMC 844
Backstitch
3 str
DMC 3740
Fur
2 str
DMC 3865
French knot
2 str
DMC 3826
Fur
2 str

STITCHING GUIDE

Stitches Used:
backstitch, fur stitch,
straight
Thread Colors:
DMC 648
DMC 646
DMC 310
DMC 3051
SIZE IN THE WILD
8"

Florida Manatee

LATIN NAME: *Trichechus manatus latirostris*

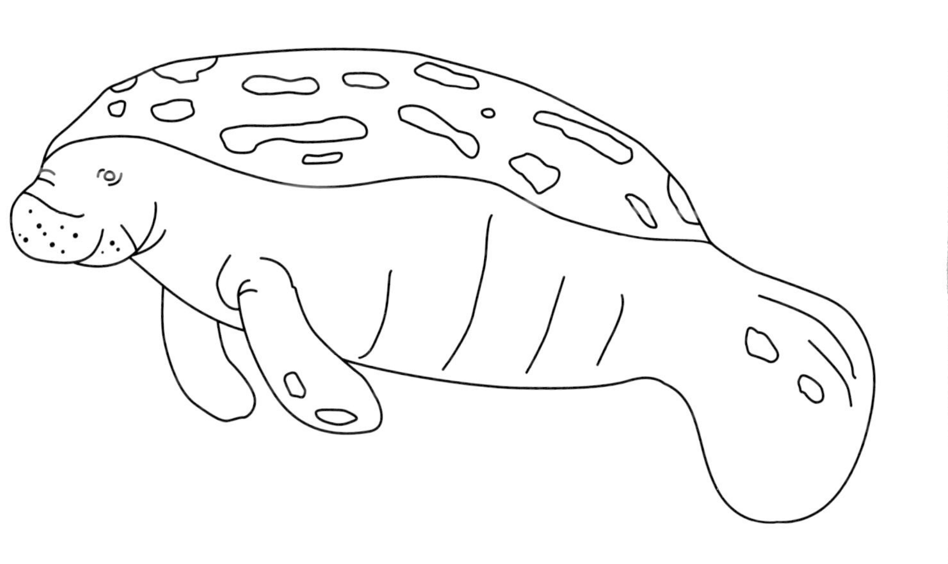

PATTERN

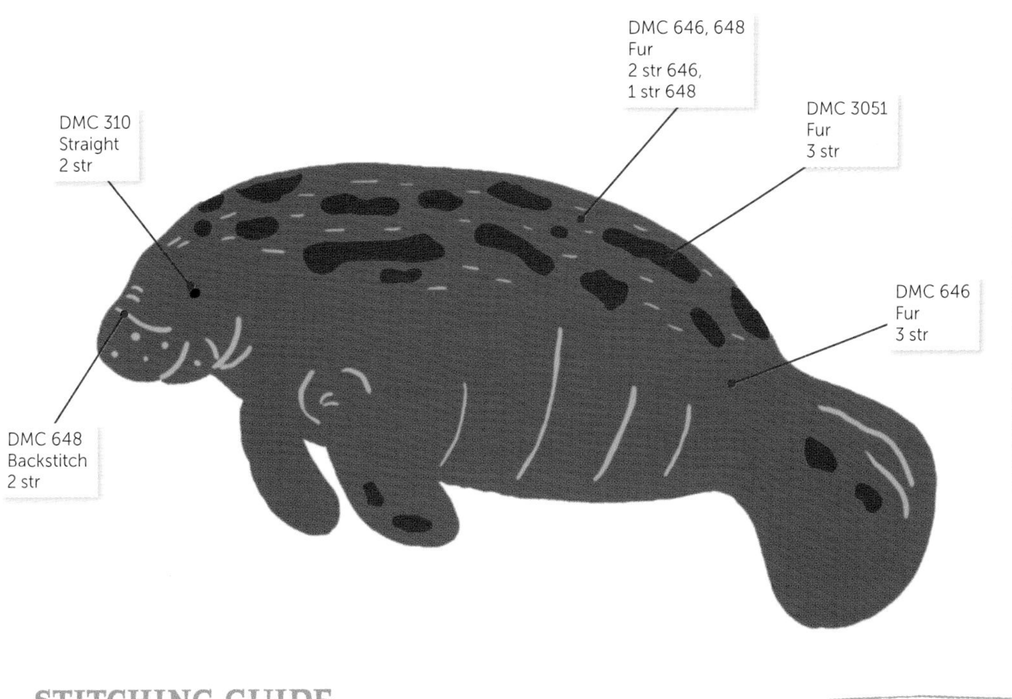
DMC 646, 648
Fur
2 str 646,
1 str 648
DMC 310
Straight
2 str
DMC 3051
Fur
3 str
DMC 646
Fur
3 str
DMC 648
Backstitch
2 str

STITCHING GUIDE

Stitches Used:
backstitch, French knot, fur stitch, straight
Thread Colors:
DMC 647
DMC 310
DMC 646
DMC 645
SIZE IN THE WILD
8"

Gray Whale

LATIN NAME: *Eschrichtius robustus*

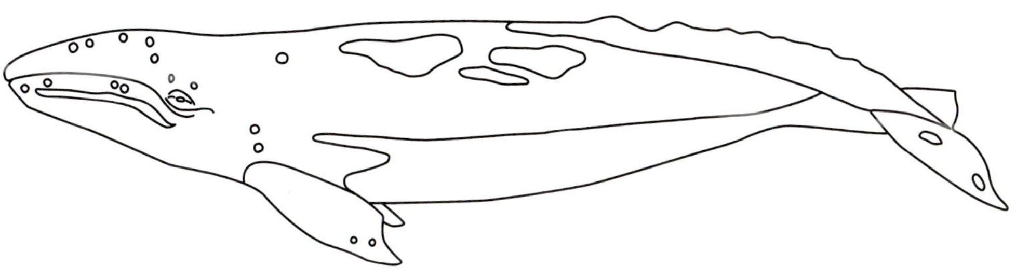

PATTERN

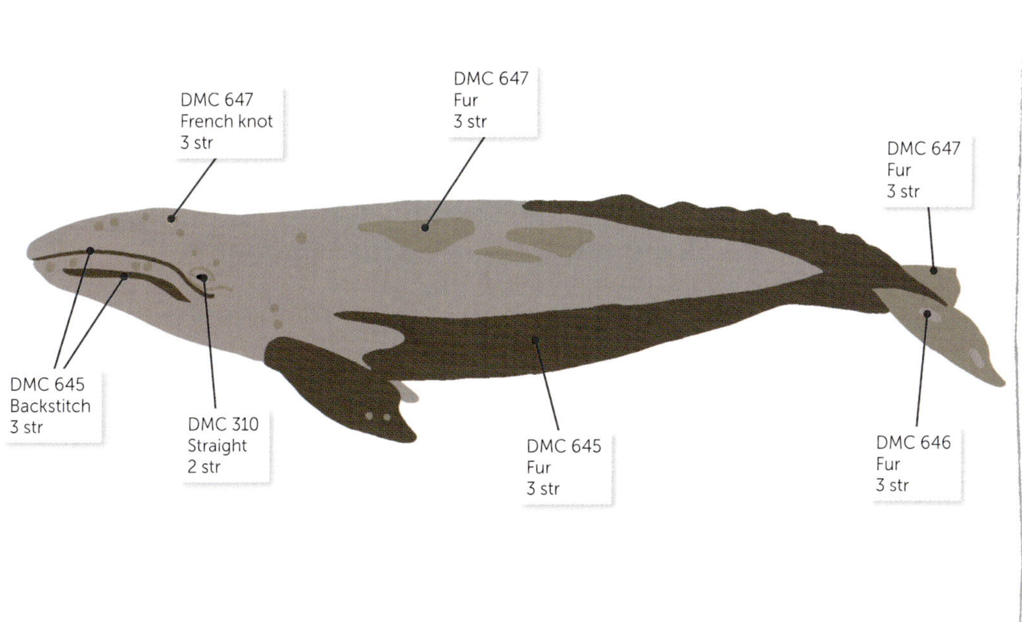

DMC 647
French knot
3 str
DMC 647
Fur
3 str
DMC 647
Fur
3 str
DMC 645
Backstitch
3 str
DMC 310
Straight
2 str
DMC 645
Fur
3 str
DMC 646
Fur
3 str

STITCHING GUIDE

Stitches Used:
backstitch, fur stitch, straight
Thread Colors:
DMC 310
DMC 167
DMC 732
DMC 3371
DMC 580
DMC 725
SIZE IN THE WILD
8"

Green Sea Turtle

LATIN NAME: *Chelonia mydas*

PATTERN

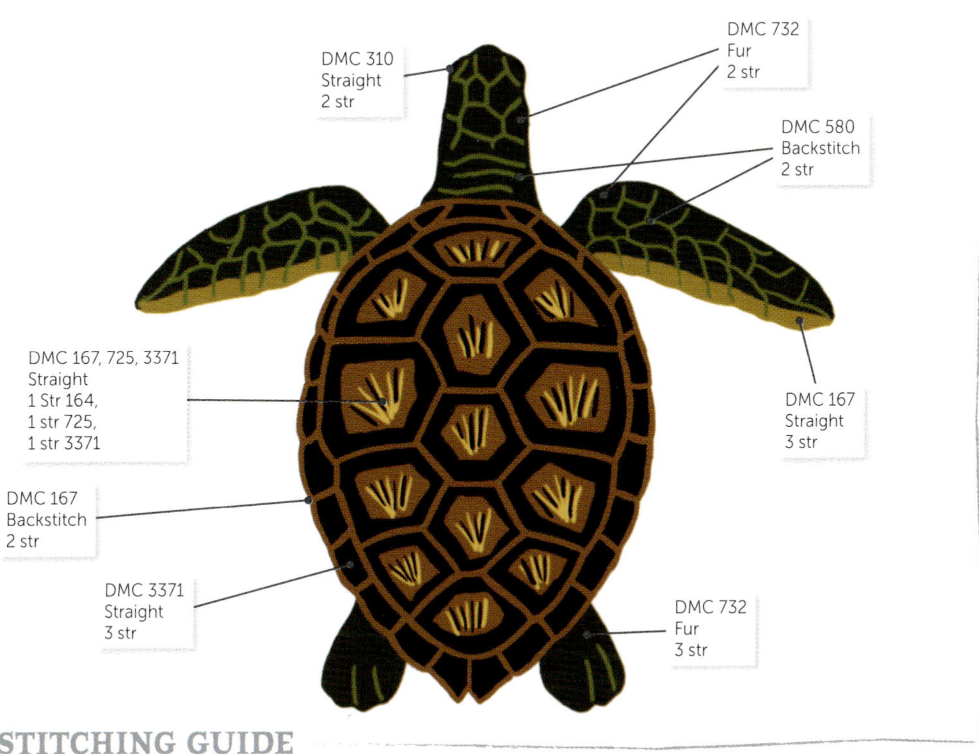
DMC 310
Straight
2 str
DMC 732
Fur
2 str
DMC 580
Backstitch
2 str
DMC 167, 725, 3371
Straight
1 Str 164,
1 str 725,
1 str 3371
DMC 167
Straight
3 str
DMC 167
Backstitch
2 str
DMC 3371
Straight
3 str
DMC 732
Fur
3 str

STITCHING GUIDE

Stitches Used:
backstitch, fur stitch, straight
Thread Colors:
DMC 535
DMC 310
DMC 646
DMC 3865
DMC 844
DMC ECRU
SIZE IN THE WILD
8"

Great White Shark

LATIN NAME: *Carcharodon carcharias*

PATTERN

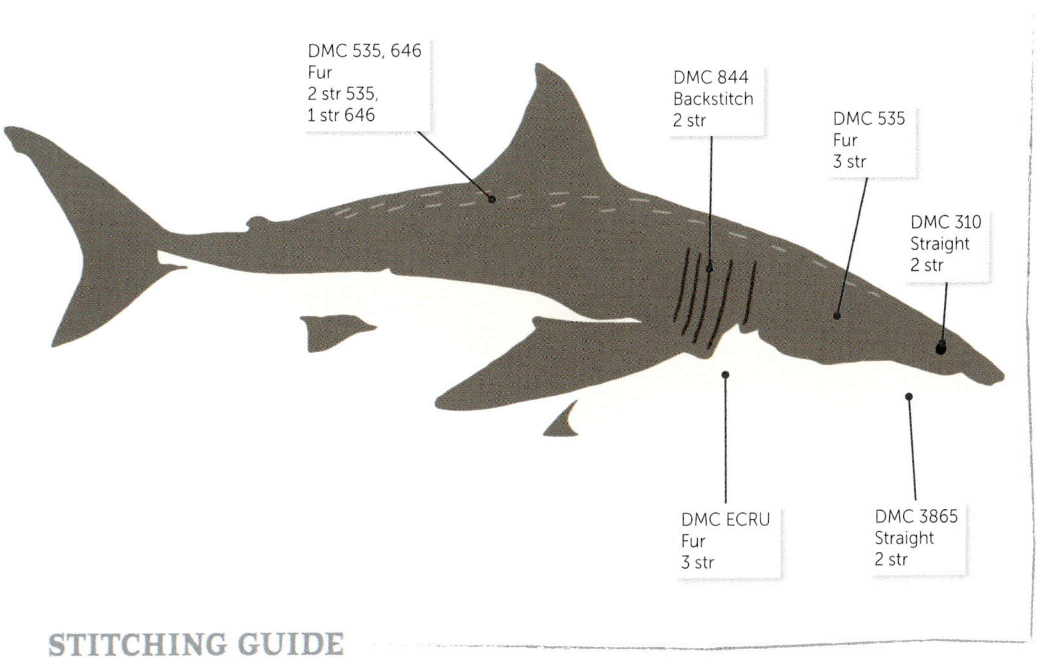
DMC 535, 646
Fur
2 str 535,
1 str 646
DMC 844
Backstitch
2 str
DMC 535
Fur
3 str
DMC 310
Straight
2 str
DMC ECRU
Fur
3 str
DMC 3865
Straight
2 str

STITCHING GUIDE

Stitches Used:
backstitch, fur stitch, straight
Thread Colors:
DMC 3821
DMC 3853
DMC 975
DMC 436
DMC 310
DMC 3799
DMC 3866
SIZE IN THE WILD
8"

Tufted Puffin

LATIN NAME: *Fratercula cirrhata*

PATTERN

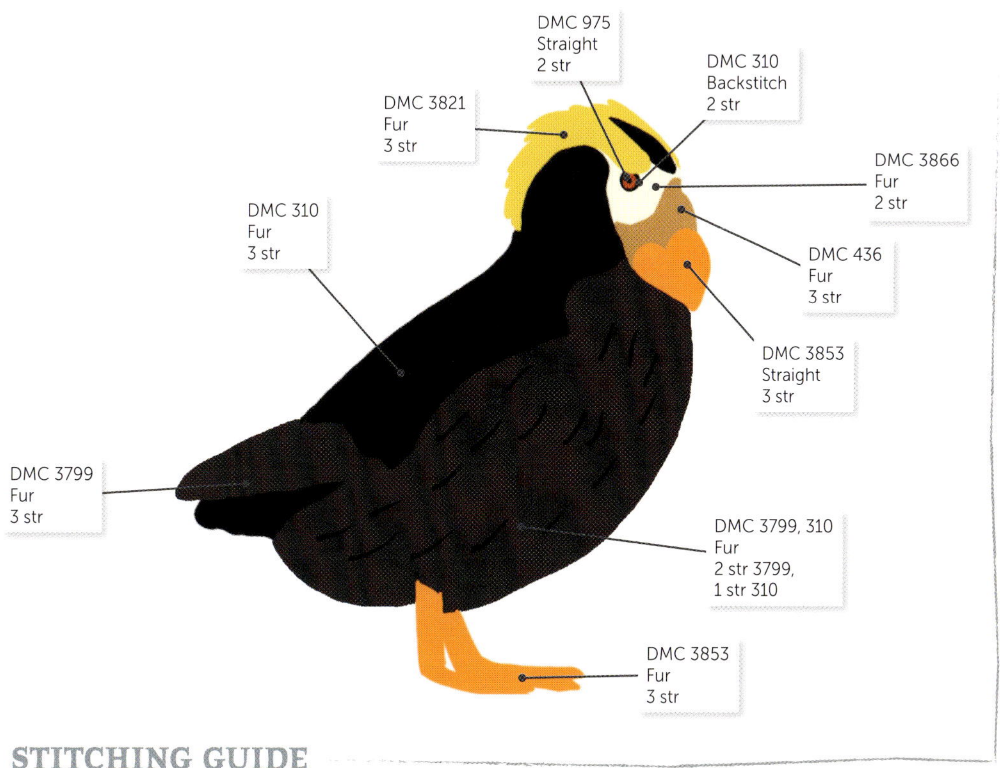
DMC 975
Straight
2 str
DMC 310
Backstitch
2 str
DMC 3821
Fur
3 str
DMC 3866
Fur
2 str
DMC 310
Fur
3 str
DMC 436
Fur
3 str
DMC 3853
Straight
3 str
DMC 3799
Fur
3 str
DMC 3799, 310
Fur
2 str 3799,
1 str 310
DMC 3853
Fur
3 str

STITCHING GUIDE

Section 6

PRAIRIE

Characterized mostly by vast open space and grasslands with fertile soils, prairies are crucial habitat for a variety of wildlife species. Although greatly altered and erased by farming and development, remaining prairies are still home to many species, including American badgers, pronghorn, and prairie dogs.

North America includes shortgrass, mixed-grass, and tallgrass prairie regions. Together, the prairie is commonly known as the Great Plains.

Stitches Used:
fur stitch, straight
Thread Colors:
DMC 433
DMC 801
DMC 780
DMC 3799
DMC 3023
DMC 310
SIZE IN THE WILD
8"

American Bison

LATIN NAME: *Bison bison*

PATTERN

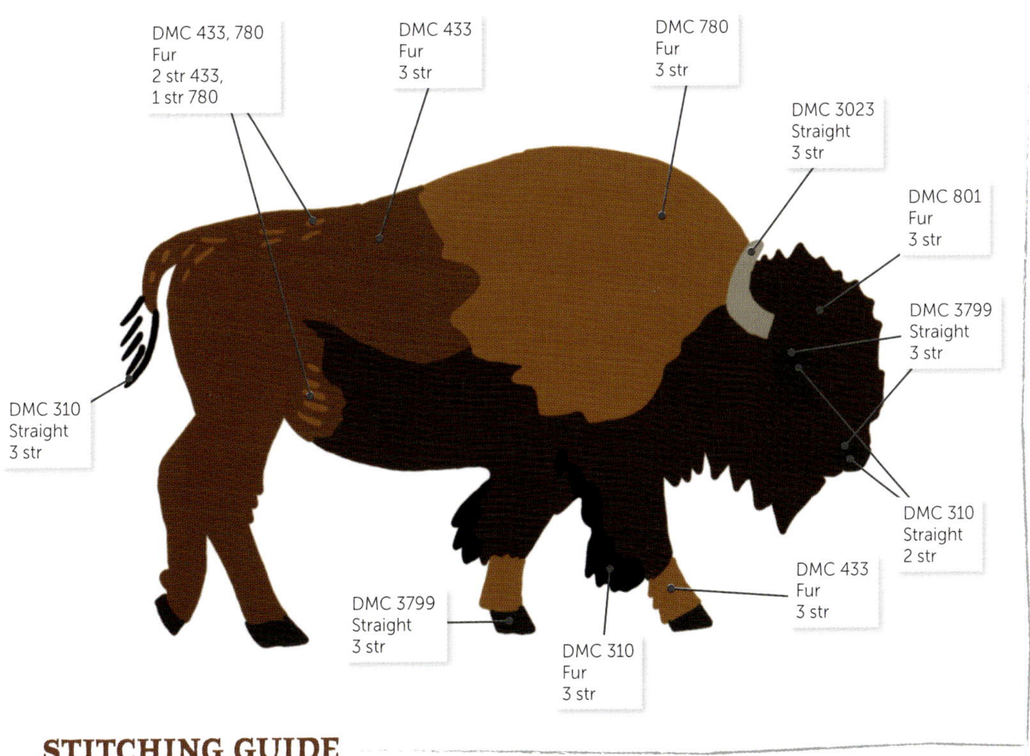
DMC 433, 780
Fur
2 str 433,
1 str 780
DMC 433
Fur
3 str
DMC 780
Fur
3 str
DMC 3023
Straight
3 str
DMC 801
Fur
3 str
DMC 3799
Straight
3 str
DMC 310
Straight
3 str
DMC 310
Straight
2 str
DMC 433
Fur
3 str
DMC 3799
Straight
3 str
DMC 310
Fur
3 str

STITCHING GUIDE

Stitches Used:
backstitch, fur stitch, straight
Thread Colors:
DMC 844
DMC 310
DMC 612
DMC ECRU
DMC 642
DMC 3346
SIZE IN THE WILD
8"

Utah Prairie Dog

LATIN NAME: *Cynomys parvidens*

PATTERN

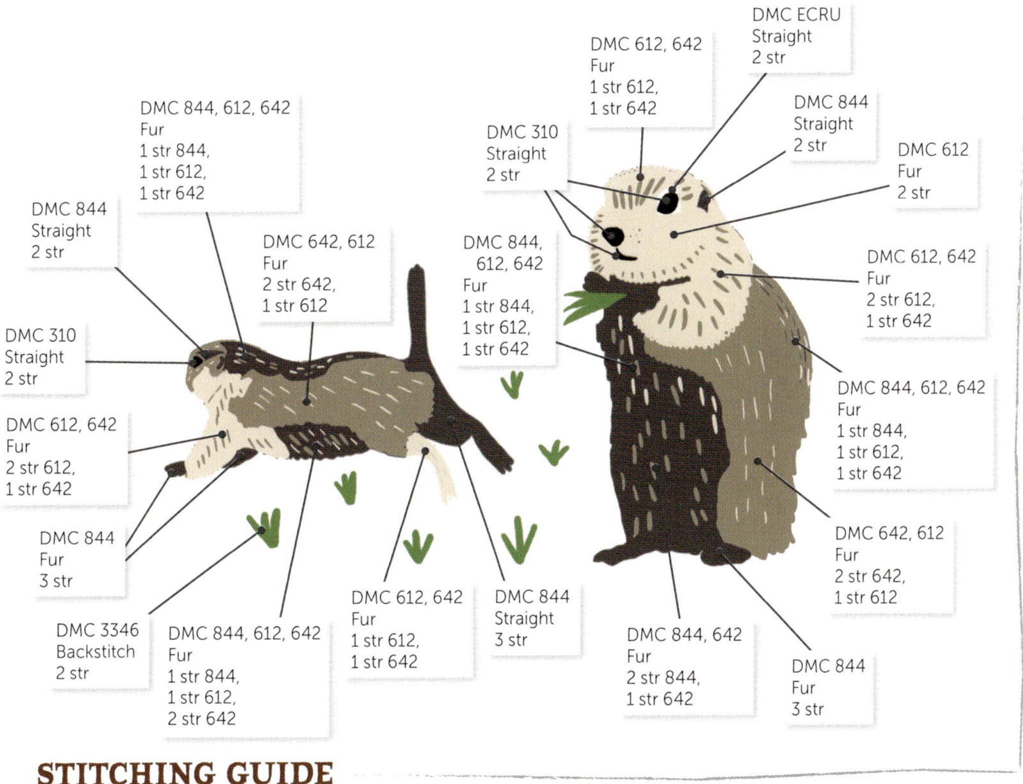
DMC ECRU
Straight
2 str
DMC 612, 642
Fur
1 str 612,
1 str 642
DMC 844
Straight
2 str
DMC 310
Straight
2 str
DMC 612
Fur
2 str
DMC 844, 612, 642
Fur
1 str 844,
1 str 612,
1 str 642
DMC 844
Straight
2 str
DMC 642, 612
Fur
2 str 642,
1 str 612
DMC 844,
612, 642
Fur
1 str 844,
1 str 612,
1 str 642
DMC 612, 642
Fur
2 str 612,
1 str 642
DMC 310
Straight
2 str
DMC 844, 612, 642
Fur
1 str 844,
1 str 612,
1 str 642
DMC 612, 642
Fur
2 str 612,
1 str 642
DMC 844
Fur
3 str
DMC 642, 612
Fur
2 str 642,
1 str 612
DMC 612, 642
Fur
1 str 612,
1 str 642
DMC 844
Straight
3 str
DMC 3346
Backstitch
2 str
DMC 844, 612, 642
Fur
1 str 844,
1 str 612,
2 str 642
DMC 844, 642
Fur
2 str 844,
1 str 642
DMC 844
Fur
3 str

STITCHING GUIDE

Stitches Used:
backstitch, fur stitch, straight
Thread Colors:
DMC ECRU
DMC 436
DMC 310
DMC 612
DMC 844
DMC 938
DMC 3045
DMC 422
SIZE IN THE WILD
8"

Black-Footed Ferret

LATIN NAME: *Mustela nigripes*

PATTERN

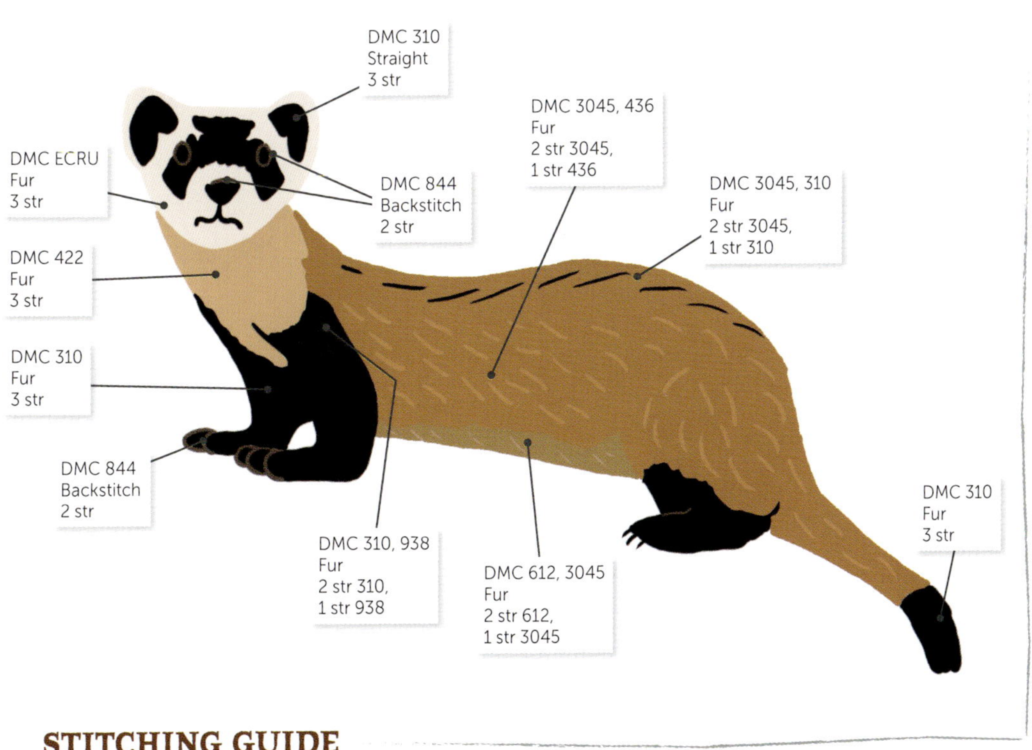
DMC 310
Straight
3 str
DMC 3045, 436
Fur
2 str 3045,
1 str 436
DMC ECRU
Fur
3 str
DMC 844
Backstitch
2 str
DMC 3045, 310
Fur
2 str 3045,
1 str 310
DMC 422
Fur
3 str
DMC 310
Fur
3 str
DMC 844
Backstitch
2 str
DMC 310
Fur
3 str
DMC 310, 938
Fur
2 str 310,
1 str 938
DMC 612, 3045
Fur
2 str 612,
1 str 3045

STITCHING GUIDE

Stitches Used:
fur stitch, straight
Thread Colors:
DMC 3865
DMC 838
DMC 310
DMC 3799
DMC 3828
DMC 648
SIZE IN THE WILD
8"

Pronghorn

LATIN NAME: *Antilocapra americana*

PATTERN

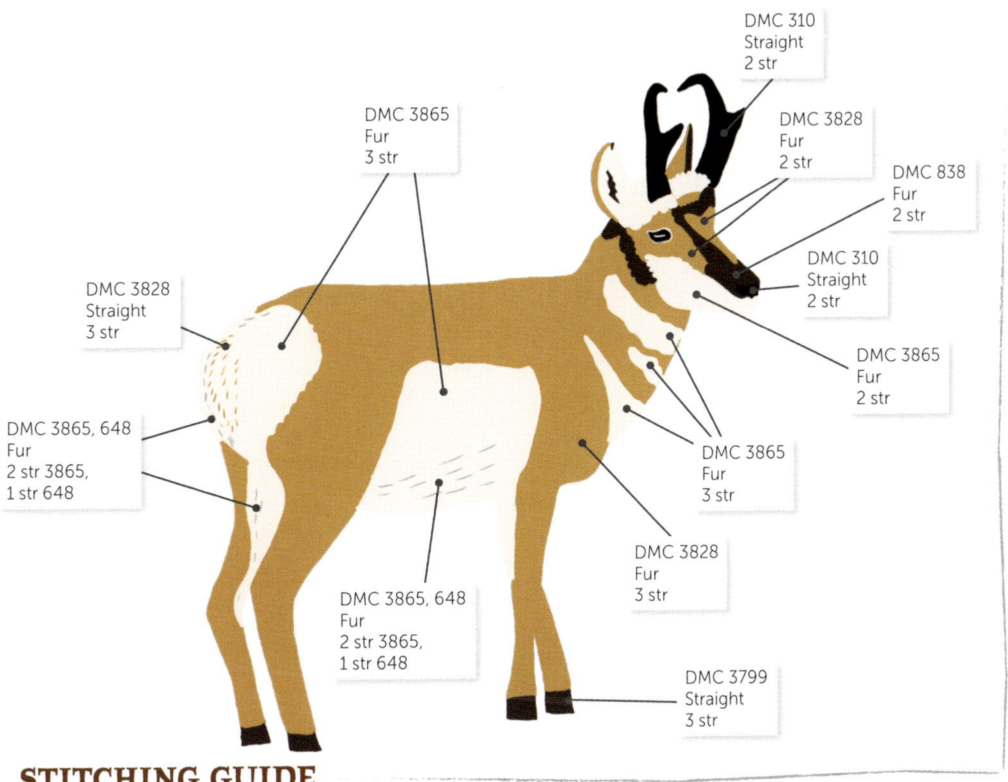
DMC 310
Straight
2 str
DMC 3865
Fur
3 str
DMC 3828
Fur
2 str
DMC 838
Fur
2 str
DMC 310
Straight
2 str
DMC 3828
Straight
3 str
DMC 3865
Fur
2 str
DMC 3865, 648
Fur
2 str 3865,
1 str 648
DMC 3865
Fur
3 str
DMC 3828
Fur
3 str
DMC 3865, 648
Fur
2 str 3865,
1 str 648
DMC 3799
Straight
3 str

STITCHING GUIDE

Stitches Used:
fur stitch, straight
Thread Colors:
DMC 310
DMC 904
DMC 844
DMC 721
DMC 3781
DMC 666
DMC 612
SIZE IN THE WILD
8"

Red-Winged Blackbird

LATIN NAME: *Agelaius phoeniceus*

PATTERN

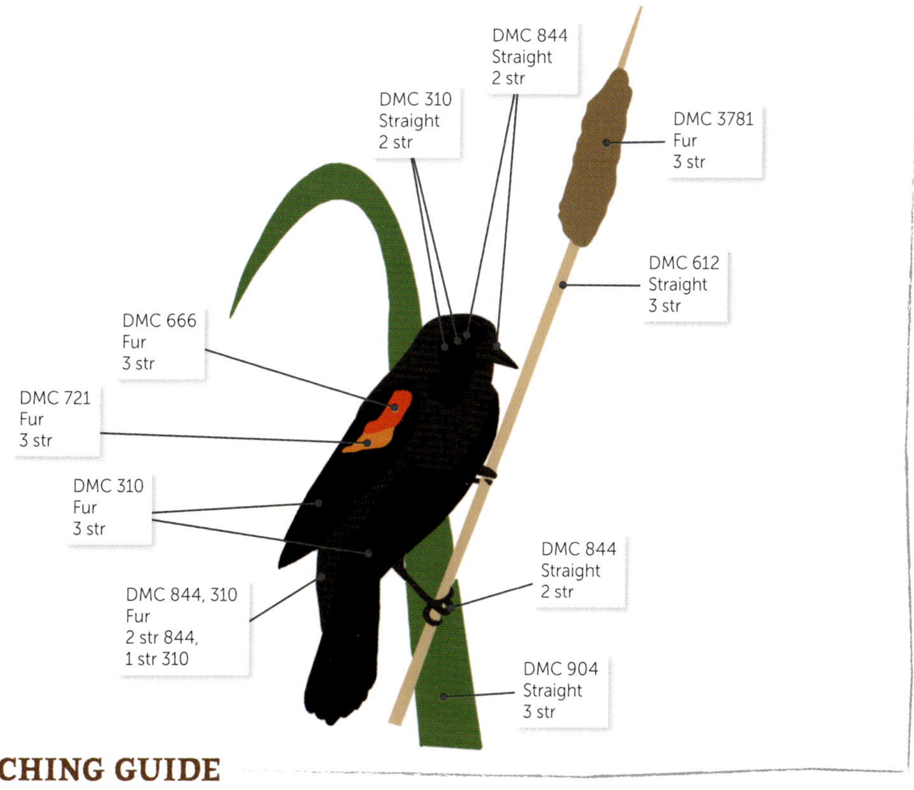

DMC 844
Straight
2 str
DMC 310
Straight
2 str
DMC 3781
Fur
3 str
DMC 612
Straight
3 str
DMC 666
Fur
3 str
DMC 721
Fur
3 str
DMC 310
Fur
3 str
DMC 844
Straight
2 str
DMC 844, 310
Fur
2 str 844,
1 str 310
DMC 904
Straight
3 str

STITCHING GUIDE

Stitches Used:
fur stitch, straight
Thread Colors:
DMC 646
DMC 310
DMC 844
DMC ECRU
DMC 422
DMC 3866
SIZE IN THE WILD
8"

American Badger

LATIN NAME: *Taxidea taxus*

PATTERN

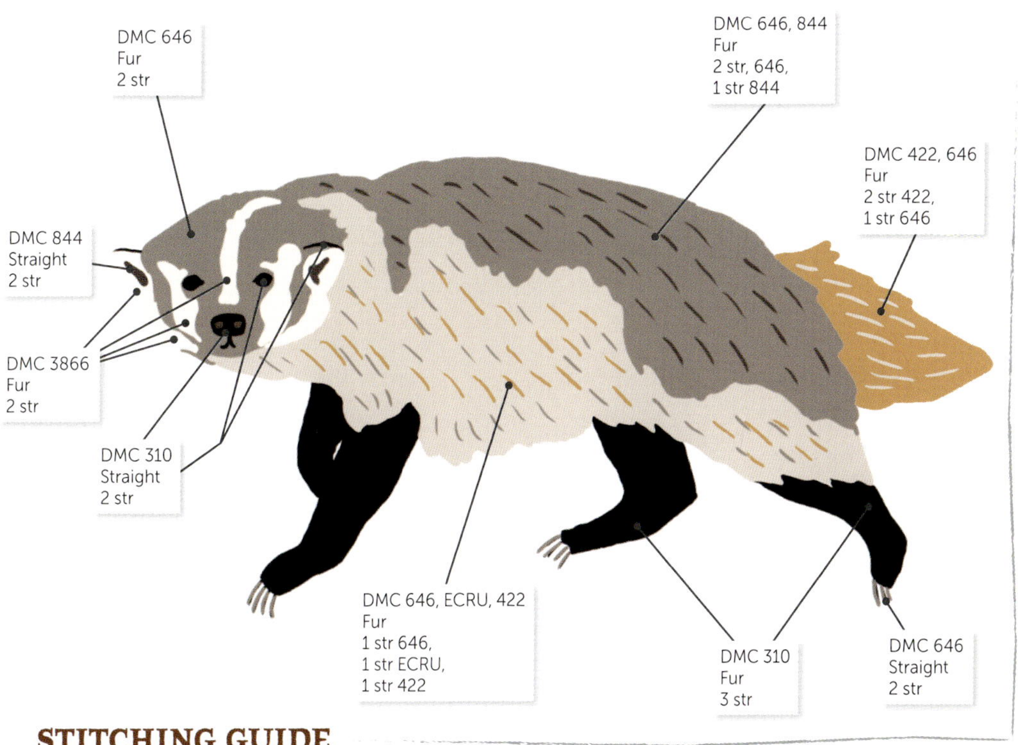
DMC 646
Fur
2 str
DMC 646, 844
Fur
2 str, 646,
1 str 844
DMC 422, 646
Fur
2 str 422,
1 str 646
DMC 844
Straight
2 str
DMC 3866
Fur
2 str
DMC 310
Straight
2 str
DMC 646, ECRU, 422
Fur
1 str 646,
1 str ECRU,
1 str 422
DMC 310
Fur
3 str
DMC 646
Straight
2 str

STITCHING GUIDE

Stitches Used:
fur stitch, straight
Thread Colors:
DMC 310
DMC 3799
DMC 3865
DMC 839
DMC 3821
DMC 829
DMC 3031
DMC 3045
SIZE IN THE WILD
8"

Greater Sage Grouse

LATIN NAME: *Centrocercus urophasianus*

PATTERN

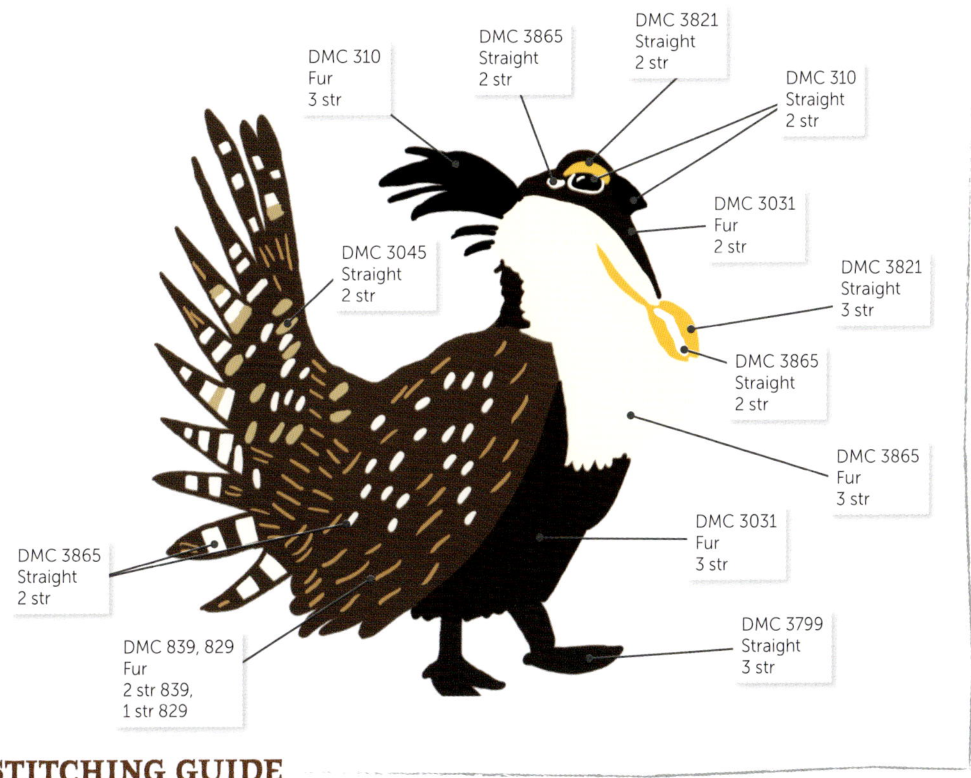
DMC 310
Fur
3 str
DMC 3865
Straight
2 str
DMC 3821
Straight
2 str
DMC 310
Straight
2 str
DMC 3031
Fur
2 str
DMC 3045
Straight
2 str
DMC 3821
Straight
3 str
DMC 3865
Straight
2 str
DMC 3865
Fur
3 str
DMC 3031
Fur
3 str
DMC 3865
Straight
2 str
DMC 3799
Straight
3 str
DMC 839, 829
Fur
2 str 839,
1 str 829

STITCHING GUIDE

Stitches Used:
backstitch, French knot, straight

Thread Colors:

DMC 921	DMC 3688
DMC 310	DMC 3820
DMC 3866	DMC 3346
DMC 3713	DMC 988

SIZE IN THE WILD

8"

Prairie Wildflower Mix

(swamp milkweed, prairie goldenrod) with monarch butterfly

LATIN NAMES: *Asclepias incarnata, Solidago nemoralis, Danaus plexippus*

PATTERN

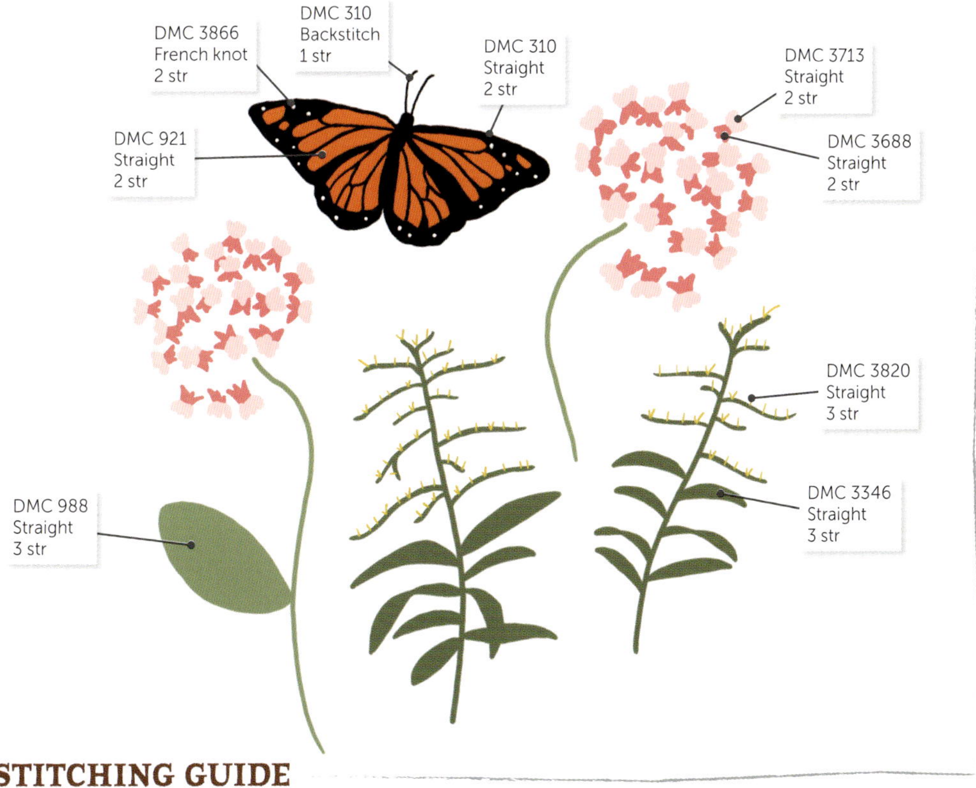

DMC 3866
French knot
2 str
DMC 310
Backstitch
1 str
DMC 310
Straight
2 str
DMC 3713
Straight
2 str
DMC 921
Straight
2 str
DMC 3688
Straight
2 str
DMC 3820
Straight
3 str
DMC 988
Straight
3 str
DMC 3346
Straight
3 str

STITCHING GUIDE

Section 7

URBAN

The urban ecosystem is especially one of a kind, partly because humans have created and transformed these spaces. Our streets, skyscraper buildings, city parks, and cemeteries sustain wildlife that have unique adaptations to living in cities, in towns, and among humans, sometimes unbeknown to us. Urban foxes, coyotes, and red-tailed hawks, among many other species, live in a variety of ecosystems but have also adapted to successfully live in urban environments.

Urban ecologists, who examine the interactions between wildlife and the human-dominated ecosystems they live in, help us find solutions to urban environmental challenges.

Stitches Used:
fur stitch, straight
Thread Colors:
DMC 844
DMC ECRU
DMC 310
DMC 646
DMC 167
DMC 975
SIZE IN THE WILD
8"

Coyote

LATIN NAME: *Canis latrans*

PATTERN

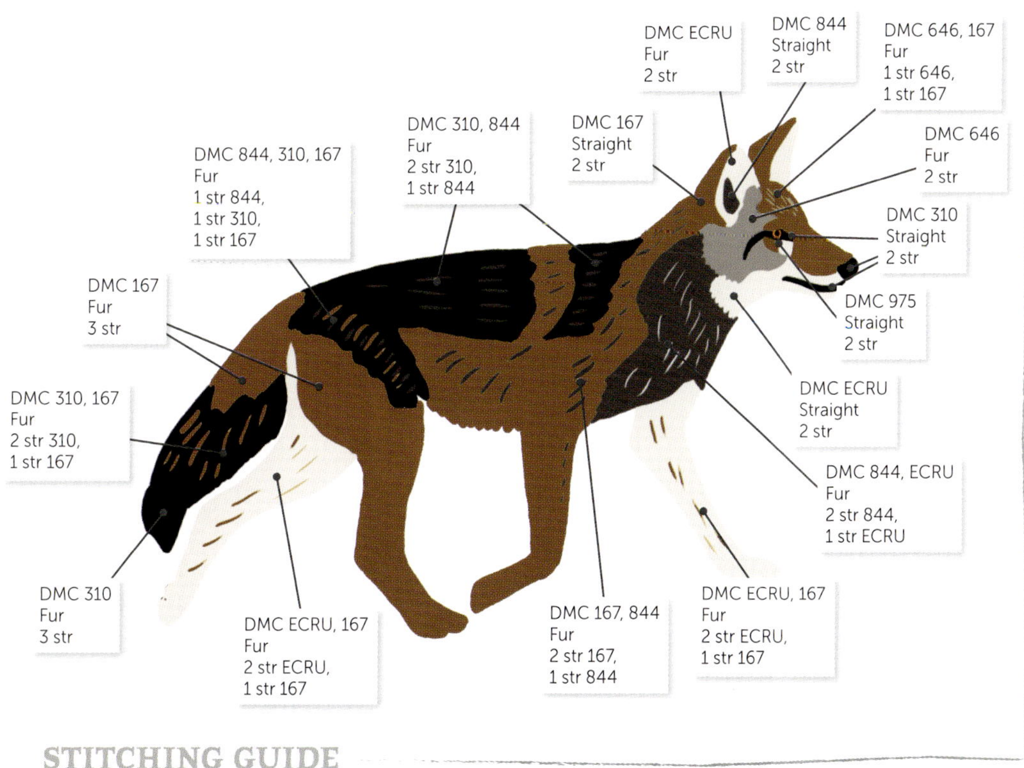
DMC ECRU
Fur
2 str
DMC 844
Straight
2 str
DMC 646, 167
Fur
1 str 646,
1 str 167
DMC 310, 844
Fur
2 str 310,
1 str 844
DMC 167
Straight
2 str
DMC 646
Fur
2 str
DMC 844, 310, 167
Fur
1 str 844,
1 str 310,
1 str 167
DMC 310
Straight
2 str
DMC 167
Fur
3 str
DMC 975
Straight
2 str
DMC 310, 167
Fur
2 str 310,
1 str 167
DMC ECRU
Straight
2 str
DMC 844, ECRU
Fur
2 str 844,
1 str ECRU
DMC 310
Fur
3 str
DMC ECRU, 167
Fur
2 str ECRU,
1 str 167
DMC 167, 844
Fur
2 str 167,
1 str 844
DMC ECRU, 167
Fur
2 str ECRU,
1 str 167

STITCHING GUIDE

Stitches Used:
fur stitch, straight
Thread Colors:
DMC 3865
DMC 03
DMC 612
DMC 646
DMC 310
DMC 844
SIZE IN THE WILD
8"

Common Raccoon

LATIN NAME: *Procyon lotor*

PATTERN

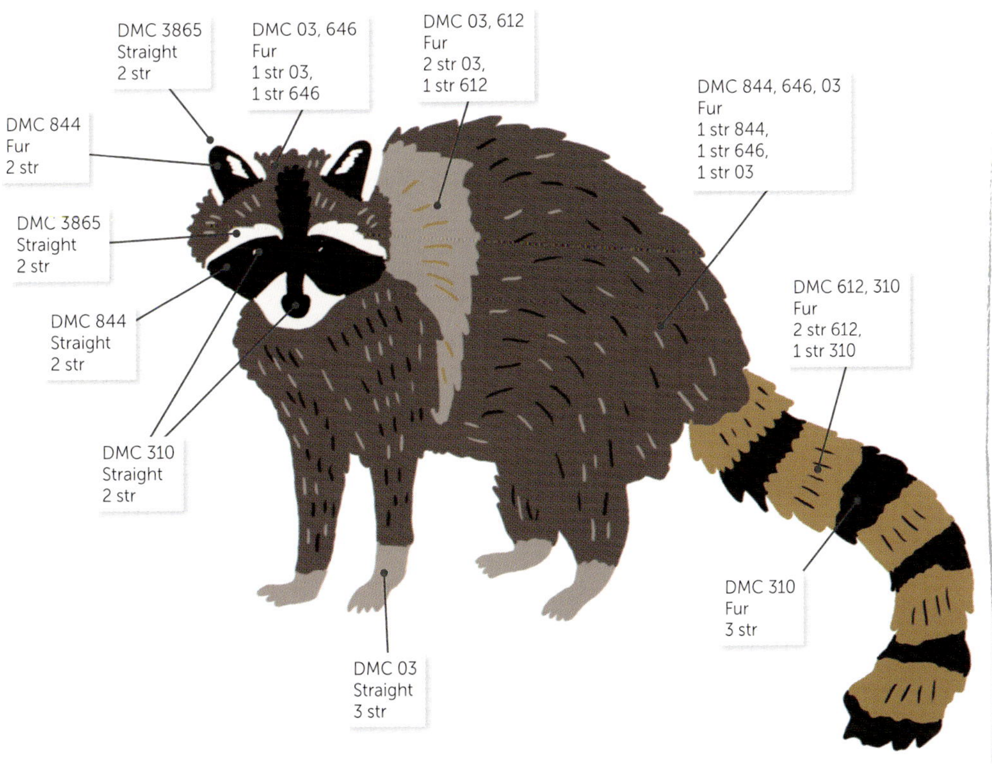
DMC 3865
Straight
2 str
DMC 03, 646
Fur
1 str 03,
1 str 646
DMC 03, 612
Fur
2 str 03,
1 str 612
DMC 844, 646, 03
Fur
1 str 844,
1 str 646,
1 str 03
DMC 844
Fur
2 str
DMC 3865
Straight
2 str
DMC 844
Straight
2 str
DMC 612, 310
Fur
2 str 612,
1 str 310
DMC 310
Straight
2 str
DMC 310
Fur
3 str
DMC 03
Straight
3 str

STITCHING GUIDE

Stitches Used:
straight
Thread Colors:
DMC 3820
DMC 781
DMC 844
DMC 310
SIZE IN THE WILD
8"

Common Garter Snake

LATIN NAME: *Thamnophis sirtalis*

PATTERN

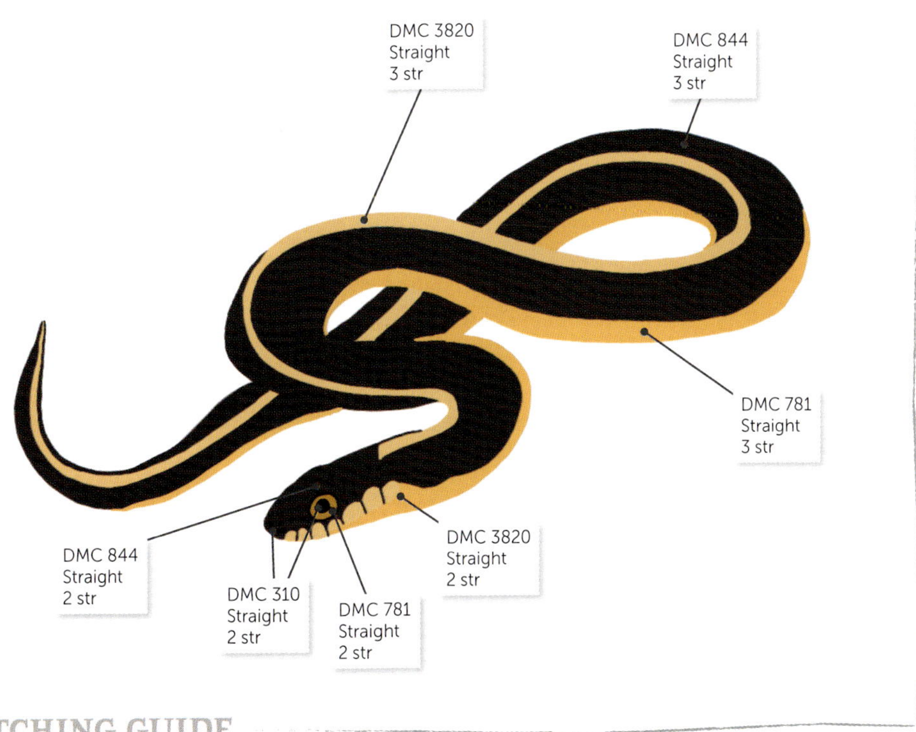
DMC 3820
Straight
3 str
DMC 844
Straight
3 str
DMC 781
Straight
3 str
DMC 844
Straight
2 str
DMC 3820
Straight
2 str
DMC 310
Straight
2 str
DMC 781
Straight
2 str

STITCHING GUIDE

Stitches Used:
fur stitch, straight
Thread Colors:
DMC 646
DMC 844
DMC 310
DMC 3865
DMC 3826
DMC 301
SIZE IN THE WILD
8"

Red Fox

LATIN NAME: *Vulpes vulpes*

PATTERN

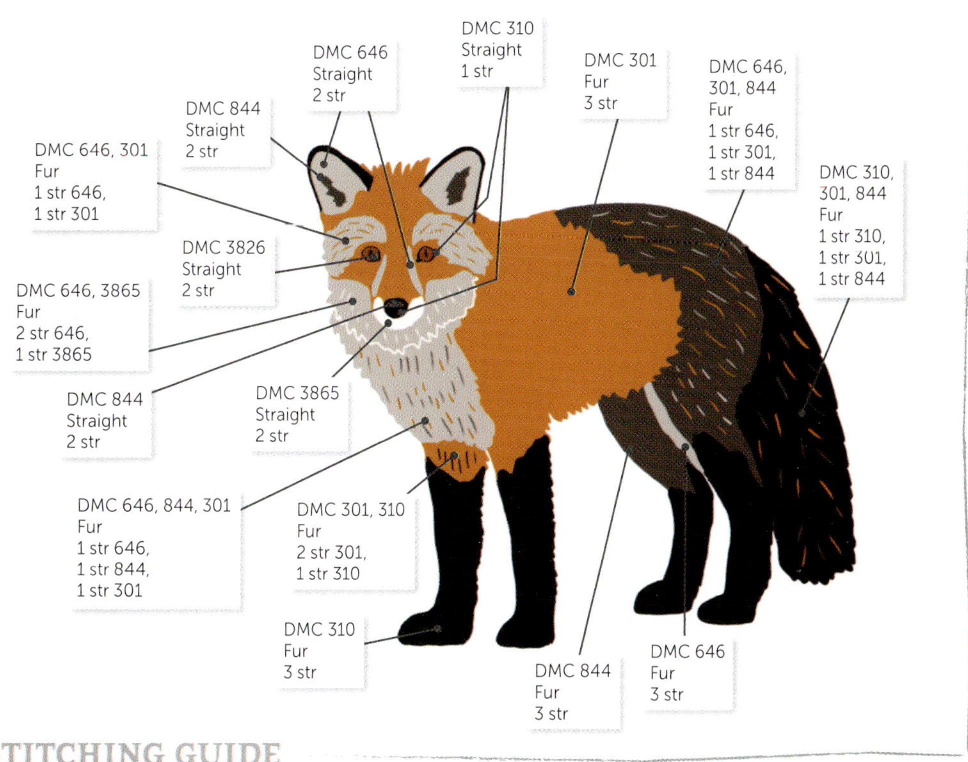
DMC 646
Straight
2 str
DMC 310
Straight
1 str
DMC 301
Fur
3 str
DMC 646,
301, 844
Fur
1 str 646,
1 str 301,
1 str 844
DMC 844
Straight
2 str
DMC 646, 301
Fur
1 str 646,
1 str 301
DMC 310,
301, 844
Fur
1 str 310,
1 str 301,
1 str 844
DMC 3826
Straight
2 str
DMC 646, 3865
Fur
2 str 646,
1 str 3865
DMC 844
Straight
2 str
DMC 3865
Straight
2 str
DMC 646, 844, 301
Fur
1 str 646,
1 str 844,
1 str 301
DMC 301, 310
Fur
2 str 301,
1 str 310
DMC 310
Fur
3 str
DMC 844
Fur
3 str
DMC 646
Fur
3 str

STITCHING GUIDE

Stitches Used:
backstitch, fur stitch, straight
Thread Colors:
DMC 3865
DMC 304
DMC 436
DMC 310
DMC ECRU
DMC 844
DMC 725
DMC 927
SIZE IN THE WILD
8"

American Herring Gull

LATIN NAME: *Larus smithsonianus*

PATTERN

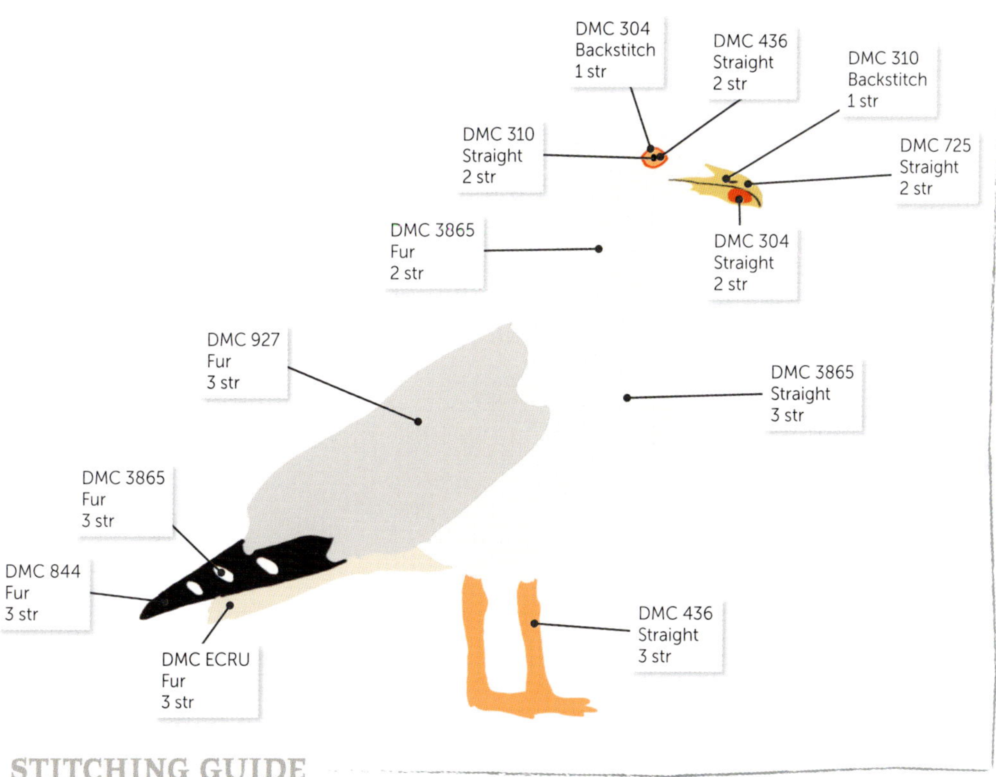

DMC 304
Backstitch
1 str
DMC 436
Straight
2 str
DMC 310
Backstitch
1 str
DMC 310
Straight
2 str
DMC 725
Straight
2 str
DMC 3865
Fur
2 str
DMC 304
Straight
2 str
DMC 927
Fur
3 str
DMC 3865
Straight
3 str
DMC 3865
Fur
3 str
DMC 844
Fur
3 str
DMC 436
Straight
3 str
DMC ECRU
Fur
3 str

STITCHING GUIDE

Stitches Used:
fur stitch, straight
Thread Colors:
DMC 310
DMC 3865
DMC 3799
SIZE IN THE WILD
8"

Striped Skunk

LATIN NAME: *Mephitis mephitis*

PATTERN

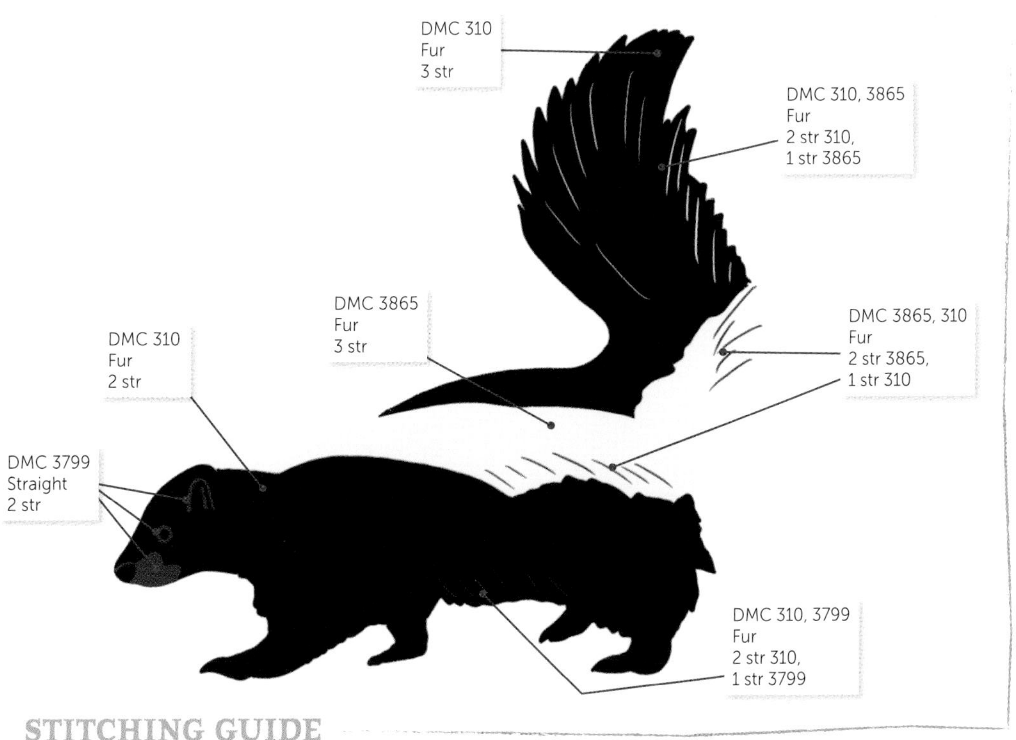
DMC 310
Fur
3 str
DMC 310, 3865
Fur
2 str 310,
1 str 3865
DMC 3865
Fur
3 str
DMC 3865, 310
Fur
2 str 3865,
1 str 310
DMC 310
Fur
2 str
DMC 3799
Straight
2 str
DMC 310, 3799
Fur
2 str 310,
1 str 3799

STITCHING GUIDE

8"

Stitches Used:
backstitch, fur stitch, straight

Thread Colors:

DMC 3820
DMC 839
DMC 310
DMC 3826
DMC 08
DMC 844
DMC ECRU
DMC 726
DMC 838

SIZE IN THE WILD

Red-Tailed Hawk

LATIN NAME: *Buteo jamaicensis*

PATTERN

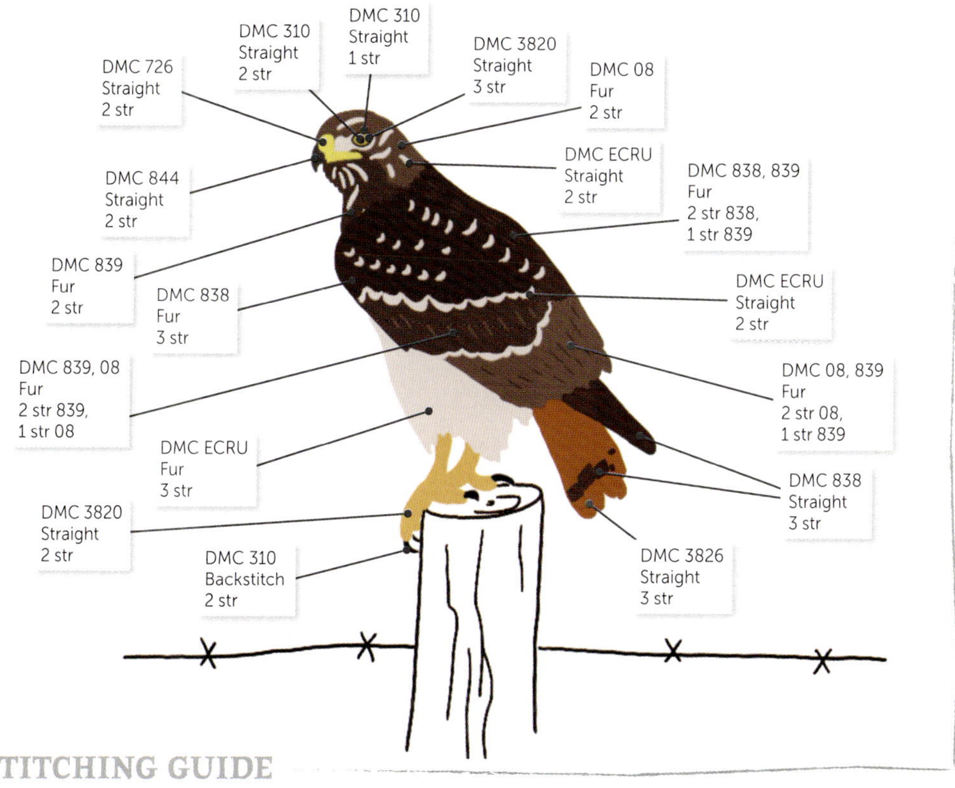
DMC 726
Straight
2 str
DMC 310
Straight
2 str
DMC 310
Straight
1 str
DMC 3820
Straight
3 str
DMC 08
Fur
2 str
DMC 844
Straight
2 str
DMC ECRU
Straight
2 str
DMC 838, 839
Fur
2 str 838,
1 str 839
DMC 839
Fur
2 str
DMC 838
Fur
3 str
DMC ECRU
Straight
2 str
DMC 839, 08
Fur
2 str 839,
1 str 08
DMC 08, 839
Fur
2 str 08,
1 str 839
DMC ECRU
Fur
3 str
DMC 838
Straight
3 str
DMC 3820
Straight
2 str
DMC 310
Backstitch
2 str
DMC 3826
Straight
3 str

STITCHING GUIDE

Jessica Kemper brings awareness to threatened species via wildlife-themed embroidery. Her business Field Guide Embroidery sells hand-embroidered goods featuring her designs, and she works to empower others to create and wear art that makes them feel connected to nature. She holds degrees in horticulture and environmental studies and has worked at zoos and conservation organizations such as the Amphibian Foundation and Tracy Aviary. Jess especially loves to take in big mountain vistas, hike, camp, bird, and check under rotting logs for slimy critters. She lives in Atlanta, Georgia, with her husband and two rescue dogs.

www.fieldguideembroidery.com
@fieldguideembroidery